DECISIONS OF THE TULLAHOMA CAMPAIGN

OTHER BOOKS IN THE COMMAND DECISIONS IN AMERICA'S CIVIL WAR SERIES

Decisions at Stones River: The Sixteen Critical Decisions That Defined the Battle
Matt Spruill and Lee Spruill

Decisions at Second Manassas: The Fourteen Critical Decisions That Defined the Battle
Matt Spruill III and Matt Spruill IV

Decisions at Chickamauga: The Twenty-Four Critical Decisions That Defined the Battle
Dave Powell

Decisions at Chattanooga: The Nineteen Critical Decisions That Defined the Battle
Larry Peterson

Decisions of the Atlanta Campaign: The Twenty-One Critical Decisions That Defined the Operation
Larry Peterson

Decisions of the 1862 Kentucky Campaign: The Twenty-Seven Critical Decisions That Defined the Operation
Larry Peterson

Decisions at Gettysburg: The Twenty Critical Decisions That Defined the Battle, Second Edition
Matt Spruill

Decisions at The Wilderness and Spotsylvania Court House: The Eighteen Critical Decisions That Defined the Battles
Dave Townsend

DECISIONS
OF THE
TULLAHOMA CAMPAIGN

The Twenty-Two Critical Decisions That Defined the Operation

Michael R. Bradley
Maps by Tim Kissel

Command Decisions
in America's Civil War

The University of Tennessee Press / Knoxville

First Edition.

All photographs are from the Library of Congress.

Library of Congress Cataloging-in-Publication Data

Names: Bradley, Michael R. (Michael Raymond), 1940- author. | Kissel, Tim, cartographer.

Title: Decisions of the Tullahoma Campaign: the twenty-two critical decisions that defined the operation / Michael R. Bradley; maps by Tim Kissel.

Other titles: Command decisions in America's Civil War.

Description: First edition. | Knoxville: The University of Tennessee Press, 2020. | Series: Command decisions in America's Civil War | Includes bibliographical references and index. | Summary: "The Tullahoma Campaign took place in Middle Tennessee between Union General Rosecrans's Army of the Cumberland and Confederate General Bragg's Army of Tennessee. Rosecrans's objective was to force the Confederate Army to vacate Middle Tennessee and threaten Chattanooga. Through a series of maneuvers, rather than battles, he achieved his goal; however, Union victories at Vicksburg and Gettysburg would overshadow his success. Decisions of the Tullahoma Campaign will be the ninth book to appear in the press's Command decisions in America's Civil War series. Books appearing in this series are geared for a general audience and offer a general introduction to the battles and campaigns of the Civil War through the lens of Union and Confederate commanders. Typical of past books in the series, the project is replete with photos and maps and includes a driving tour of the decisions to encourage visitation to National Battlefield Parks."— Provided by publisher.

Identifiers: LCCN 2020004171 (print) | LCCN 2020004172 (ebook) | ISBN 9781621905660 (paperback) | ISBN 9781621905677 (Kindle edition) | ISBN 9781621905684 (Adobe PDF)

Subjects: LCSH: Tullahoma Campaign, 1863. | Command of troops—Case studies. | Tennessee, Middle—History, Military—19th century. | Tullahoma (Tenn.)—History, Military—19th century.

Classification: LCC E475.16 .B725 2020 (print) | LCC E475.16 (ebook) | DDC 973.7/34—dc23

LC record available at https://lccn.loc.gov/2020004171

LC ebook record available at https://lccn.loc.gov/2020004172

CONTENTS

ILLUSTRATIONS

Figures

Maps

PREFACE

The overall purpose of this book is to help the reader gain a clearer understanding of the importance of the Tullahoma Campaign and its effect on later campaigns, such as Chickamauga and Atlanta.

The Tullahoma Campaign took place during the last week of June and the first four days of July 1863, the same time the siege of Vicksburg was reaching a climax and the Battle of Gettysburg was being fought. Thousands of Confederates were captured at Vicksburg, and thousands of Union and Confederate soldiers became casualties at Gettysburg. Rosecrans accomplished his objective with fewer than one thousand men killed and wounded, and so his victory was obscured by the more dramatic events in Mississippi and Pennsylvania. But the results of the Tullahoma Campaign were of great importance in helping the United States gain the ultimate victory of restoring the Union.

At the time of the Civil War, accepted military doctrine held that an army needed to achieve the following objectives to emerge victorious: occupy enemy territory permanently, deprive opponents of food supplies, deprive opponents of recruits, deprive opponents of transportation facilities, and deprive opponents of industrial capacity. Many general officers were still guided by the older concept that destruction of the enemy army provided the path to victory. The criteria stated above constituted military thinkers' "modern" ideas.

At Gettysburg, the Army of the Potomac under Gen. George Mead provided an enormous psychological boost to the Union war effort. This effect should not be discounted—the battle was the Army of the Potomac's first victory, and it was won on "home soil" in the North. Also, the process of attrition that finally depleted Confederate manpower reserves began at Gettysburg. But Gettysburg was a defensive victory for the United States forces, and the immediate aftermath of the battle returned Virginia to the status quo. The fruits of the Union victory at Gettysburg would take a long time to ripen.

Vicksburg brought economic and political benefits to the Lincoln administration by opening the route by which midwestern farmers sent their grain to market. As long as the Mississippi River was closed to commercial traffic, grain crops from the Midwest had to depend on two railroads, the Baltimore & Ohio and the New York Central, to haul their crops to market. The B&O was an unreliable route through territory that was sometimes controlled by the Confederates and at other times susceptible to raids from Southern forces. The NYC could not handle the amount of traffic the farmers produced, making navigation of the Mississippi crucial. Once Vicksburg was captured, midwestern grain could reach Europe and the East Coast of the United States. Solving this economic problem also lessened the appeal of antiwar groups. A series of resolutions adopted by the Minnesota legislature on January 19, 1861, illustrates the economic motive for the Union's military focus on Vicksburg. The seventh of these resolutions reads, "Resolved: That we never will consent or submit to the obstruction of the free navigation of the Mississippi River, from its source to its mouth, by any power hostile to the Federal Government."[1]

While many students of the Civil War argue that the fall of Vicksburg deprived the Confederates of necessary supplies, the argument will not stand scrutiny. The Confederacy survived the loss of Vicksburg because very little in the way of manpower or supplies was crossing the Mississippi from the west. Neither did the capture of Vicksburg give the US forces control of farmland, pools of recruits, vital transportation networks, or industrial capacity. Soon after its capture, Vicksburg became a backwater from which no major US campaign was mounted, with the single exception of Sherman's Meridian Campaign.

The Mississippi Central Railroad and the Mobile & Ohio Railroad continued to provide transportation for the Confederacy until the end of the war. Confederate recruits were gathered in by Nathan Bedford Forrest and his subordinate commanders until the collapse of the Confederacy. Mississippi continued to supply food to the Army of Tennessee throughout the Atlanta Campaign and to local Confederate forces until the end of the fighting. As for industry, there was none in the area. Many of the men who surrendered to Grant at Vicksburg in July were back in the ranks and fighting Rosecrans at Chickamauga in September. Thus Grant's victory at Vicksburg gave a psychological boost to the US war effort and helped the Lincoln administration both economically and politically, but it was of limited value militarily.

In the Tullahoma Campaign, William S. Rosecrans achieved objectives of immediate value to the Union. The fertile food-producing land of Middle Tennessee was permanently lost to the Confederacy, and a deep pool of recruits was abandoned (and many from the area already in the ranks began to desert). Important transportation facilities came under US control, and these facilities provided the support for Sherman's Atlanta Campaign the following year. Finally, the Southern war effort lost factories that provided a great deal of cloth, iron, and gunpowder.

Rosecrans's success in the Tullahoma Campaign shifted the focus of the Union war effort from the Mississippi River area to the corridor traversed by the Nashville & Chattanooga Railroad and the Western & Atlantic Railroad. General Sherman would follow this route to Atlanta in 1864. Although largely lost sight of, Rosecrans brought the US closer to a final victory, and his efforts should not be overlooked for Meade's and Grant's.

My knowledge about what happened in the Tullahoma Campaign, developed in the research already described, led me to ask another question—Why did the campaign happen? The methodology for answering this question involves examining critical decisions. This type of analysis allows someone who has an understanding of "what happened" to move to the next level and ask why something happened and what caused it. When the critical-decision concept is understood, it can be applied to any battle or campaign in any war.

During the Tullahoma Campaign events occurred as they did because of the decisions made at all levels of command on both sides of the conflict. Clearly, both Rosecrans and Bragg made a number of choices during the six-month period between the end of the Battle of Stones River and the beginning of the Tullahoma Campaign. Some decisions were the normal ones made during any campaign or battle. Others, however, were more important. I wanted to know what decisions were so crucial that they influenced the rest of the campaign, shaping the way that it unfolded. These were the critical decisions.

Critical decisions cover the entire spectrum of war: strategy, operations, tactics, and organization. Some decisions that initially appear to be minor ultimately become critical and have a major impact on subsequent events. It is important that you, the reader, understand the concept of a critical decision. Without this understanding this book will appear to be only a short and select narrative of events during the Tullahoma Campaign. This work is not intended as such. It employs the new concept of exploring why battles and campaigns developed as they did—the *why* instead of the *what.*

A hierarchy of decisions may be illustrated as follows:

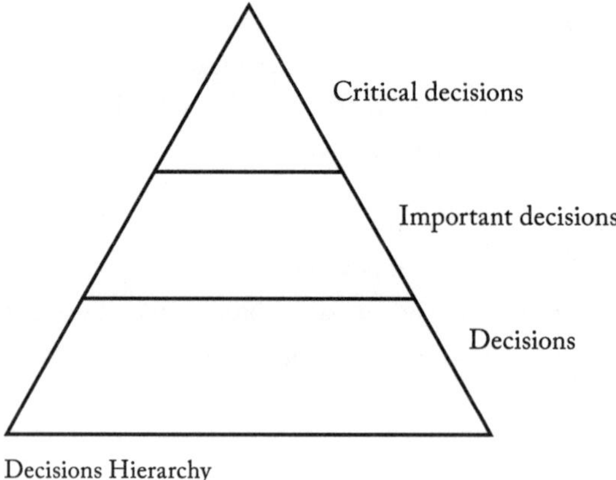

Decisions Hierarchy

At the bottom of the hierarchy are the many and varied decisions that must be made in a campaign or battle. Then come important decisions that have some effect on the outcome of the event. The few critical decisions that would have changed the entire course of the campaign had they been decided differently occupy the top of the hierarchy.

The criterion for a critical decision is that its magnitude shaped the events that followed and the campaign from that point onward. If these critical decisions had not been made, or if a different decision had been made, subsequent events in the Tullahoma Campaign would have been significantly different, perhaps even altering the course of the war.

As the aforementioned hierarchy indicates, some decisions were the sort that any commander would have made in any campaign. Others were more significant, influencing the outcome of a skirmish or deciding the direction taken by a major unit of the army for a day or so. Even so, these choices had limited influence on the troops' operations. Those critical decisions that shaped the development and outcome of the Tullahoma Campaign need to be examined and, along with their results, analyzed from an accurately focused historical viewpoint.

This is not another history of the Tullahoma Campaign covering all the events of the ten days of operations and the six months leading up to them. Readers who need such information should consult one of the sources listed in the endnotes.[2] There they will find detailed narratives of the campaign and varied interpretations as to its meaning. This book concentrates on the critical decisions and presents some basic facts providing a relatively clear view of a complex situation. Without neglecting important details, this account offers the reader a coherent and manageable blueprint as to why the campaign developed as it did.

The criteria for defining these critical decisions have been developed by Larry Peterson in his *Decisions at Chattanooga*, by Matt Spruill and Lee Spruill in their *Decisions at Stones River*, and by Matt Spruill and Matt Spruill IV in their *Decisions at Second Manassas*.[3] The authors state that a critical decision impacts events directly following it as well as the subsequent course of the fighting. Without these critical decisions the sequence of events for the entire campaign would have been different. Some of these decisions were easily reached because of the nature of existing conditions such as road networks, but others were reached with more difficulty and required analysis and evaluation of changing conditions.

Two commanding officers located in separate towns made the critical decisions that determined the course of the Tullahoma Campaign. William S. Rosecrans led the Army of the Cumberland from his headquarters in Murfreesboro, Tennessee, while Braxton Bragg oversaw the Army of Tennessee at his headquarters in Tullahoma, about forty miles east and south of Murfreesboro. The generals were both guided and hampered in their decision-making by directions received from their respective war departments. Moreover, both had to deal with dissension in the ranks of their commands, and both were at the mercy of the weather. In many cases, the importance of what proved to be a critical decision took several weeks to emerge.

Most Civil War battles lasted only one day, a few two or three. Other than during sieges, officers had to make critical decisions rapidly during combat. This book deals with a different situation—a ten-day campaign preceded by six months of preparation for action. The officers involved had time to consider their options and review their decisions before implementing them.

Little combat occurred during the Tullahoma Campaign; therefore, this work contains no discussion of critical decisions made on the battlefield. The ten days of the campaign were filled with maneuvers in which soldiers shed a great deal of sweat but spilled very little blood. The weather did play a major role in the campaign, as it rained heavily at some point during each of the ten days. This rainfall deteriorated the roads so seriously that some units found maneuvering impossible.

The critical decisions discussed in this book concern strategy, operations, tactics, organizations, logistics, and personnel. Of the decisions reached during the Tullahoma Campaign, two were strategic, two were tactical, one was logistical, and one concerned personnel. Organizational concerns played a role in some of these determinations but was not the major factor in any of them.

Furthermore, the critical decisions affecting the Tullahoma Campaign occurred in three distinct time periods—before, during, and following the campaign.

Before the Campaign

- Bragg Holds the Line of the Duck River—January 5
- Rosecrans Secures His Line of Supply—January 11
- Rosecrans Strengthens His Cavalry—January 14
- Rosecrans Creates a Mounted Infantry Force—February 16
- Bragg Arrests Gen. John McCown—February 18
- Wilder Equips His Command with Technologically Advanced Rifles—March 20
- Rosecrans Uses His Mounted Infantry Against John Hunt Morgan's Position—April 2
- Jefferson Davis and Bragg Disperse Men from the Army of Tennessee—May 23
- No Replacement Is Named When Forrest Is Disabled—June 14
- Bragg Strips His Right Flank of Cavalry—June 14–20

During the Campaign

- Wilder Disregards Orders to Fall Back and Holds the Mouth of Hoover's Gap—June 23
- Rosecrans Alters His Plan to Adapt to the Changed Circumstances—June 25
- Bragg Evacuates Shelbyville—June 27
- Rosecrans Does Not Pause at Manchester but Continues to Maneuver—June 27
- Bragg Evacuates Tullahoma—June 30
- Bragg Abandons Middle Tennessee—July 2–3

Following the Campaign

- Rosecrans Pauses to Refit and Resupply His Army—July 10
- Bragg Opts to Remain on the Defensive—July 13

These decisions were not divinely foreordained; either commanding general could have made other choices at any point. Had other determinations been reached, the results of the campaign might well have been different and the future of the entire war altered. For example, had Rosecrans been stopped or forced back to Murfreesboro, there would have been no Battle of Chickamauga. In addition, the Atlanta Campaign of 1864 would have started from Middle Tennessee instead of Dalton, Georgia, and the capture of Atlanta might not have taken place prior to the November 1864 elections. It is not the purpose of this book to present an alternative history. However, readers can apply their minds to visualizing that the results of the Tullahoma Campaign, and the war, were not inevitable. They were the result of critical decisions. This work is an invitation to think about the Tullahoma Campaign, and all other Civil War campaigns, in a different way. In addition to learning what happened, ask why something happened.

In reading about the Tullahoma Campaign, you will notice familiar troop designations identifying a regiment by a number followed by a state (Twentieth Tennessee, Seventy-Second Indiana), as well as some units identified as "regular army troops." A battalion of US Regulars fought at Hoover's Gap. These men enlisted in the US Army and not in state formations were "on loan" to the volunteer forces of the United States. On the Confederate side some units were identified by a number followed by "Confederate" (Eighth Confederate Cavalry). Whenever a single state could not supply enough men to form a regiment, the Confederate government combined troops from several states into a unit that was part of the national standing army, not the provisional army of volunteers.

There is always value in being in close proximity to the ground where a decision was made or carried out. When present at such a location, students of the campaign can see the terrain and the tactical situation as the decision-maker did, thereby gaining important insight. The Tullahoma Campaign presents something of a challenge—Rosecrans was making decisions in Murfreesboro, Bragg was making decisions forty miles away in Tullahoma, and still other decisions were reached in Washington or Richmond. However, it is possible to visit the locations where most of the critical decisions for the campaign were made or implemented. In addition, an appendix contains a driving tour that will place the reader at, or near, the ground on which a critical decision was made or carried out. This tour includes excerpts from the *Official Records* and from the letters and diaries of soldiers who fought in the campaign. By visiting the tour stops, readers who have informed themselves about the events of the Tullahoma Campaign can better appreciate its importance and the effects of its critical decisions.

While urban growth or highway construction has altered some of the terrain, much of the landscape of the Tullahoma Campaign remains relatively intact. Those who want to see the ground over which the operations were conducted can visit the area to gain a good idea of the prevailing conditions in 1863. Fortress Rosecrans has been preserved in a city park in Murfreesboro. Several buildings associated with the Army of the Cumberland's period of occupation still stand and are open to the public. The construction of Interstate 24 affected Hoover's Gap, one of the locations where combat did occur, and towns in the area have grown. Yet much of the terrain the armies covered during the Tullahoma Campaign is largely unchanged. While both Rosecrans and Bragg made critical decisions during the campaign, the relevant area is most easily toured by following the routes US forces took to reach the points Confederate forces defended.

I have lived in Tullahoma, Tennessee, since 1970 and am surrounded by physical reminders of the Tullahoma Campaign. For thirty-six years I drove to work at Motlow College, passing earthworks the Army of Tennessee erected to defend the town. Yet like most historians of the Civil War, I ignored the importance of the events that had produced these reminders.

I first began to focus on the Tullahoma Campaign in 1995, when a local tourism group asked me to compose a brochure to be given to vacationers interested in Civil War history. It was hoped that this publication would convince some of those visiting Stones River Battlefield to stop in Tullahoma as they drove east to visit Chickamauga. While writing the brochure, I was struck by the fact that I was having to do all my research in primary sources. No secondary account of the Tullahoma Campaign was available at that time.

As a result, I wrote *Tullahoma: The 1863 Campaign for the Control of Middle Tennessee,* published in 2000. That effort convinced me that the Tullahoma Campaign was much more important than historians had generally recognized. Prior to 2000 the Tullahoma Campaign had been dealt with only briefly by Thomas Lawrence Connelly in *Autumn of Glory,* Benjamin Franklin Cooling in *Fort Donelson's Legacy,* and Steven Woodworth in *Six Armies in Tennessee.* More recently, Christopher Kolakowski devoted a chapter to Tullahoma in *The Stones River and Tullahoma Campaigns.* Combined, the works by Connelly, Cooling, and Woodworth devote fewer than two dozen pages to the campaign, while Kolakowski's study gives more description and some analysis. One purpose of this book is to call attention to what has been a neglected Civil War campaign and its results.

INTRODUCTION

The tactical victory won by William S. Rosecrans at Murfreesboro had been a boon to the Lincoln administration. The Battle of Stones River on the last day of December 1862 and the first two days of January 1863 had reversed a long, depressing string of failures and reverses for Lincoln and the Union cause. The year had begun promisingly, with Gen. Ulysses Grant driving deep into the Confederate heartland following his victories at Fort Henry and Fort Donelson. The Confederate counterattack at Shiloh had been repulsed, but the war in the West slowed to a crawl following that battle. Gen. Henry Halleck replaced Grant in field command, and the Union army crept very slowly toward Corinth. On the Confederate side, the evacuation of Corinth had brought a change in command as Gen. Braxton Bragg replaced Gen. Pierre Beauregard.

Though often maligned as a field commander, Bragg was an excellent administrator, and he brought much-needed organization and discipline to his men. Bragg was also an excellent strategist. He had used the railroad network to move his army from northern Mississippi to Chattanooga, and he had then made a sudden strike north and west into Kentucky. This move forced the Union armies to abandon much of the territory they had occupied in the spring of 1862.

The war in the East had also been one of wide swings of fortune for the North. While the spring had opened with McClelland's army within sight of the church spires of Richmond, September found Confederates in Maryland.

Braxton Bragg.

Of even greater importance, the wounding of Gen. Joseph Johnston led to Robert E. Lee's promotion to command the force he would name the Army of Northern Virginia. During the Seven Days' Battles, Lee forced McClellan to retreat to a safe post on the James River. Washington officials recalled the army to the Potomac River from this location. During the interval while McClellan was in transit, Lee smashed the newly created Army of Virginia commanded by Gen. John Pope and undertook an incursion into Maryland. Bloody fighting at Antietam Creek, near the town of Sharpsburg, forced Lee to return to Virginia, but three months later he inflicted a bloody repulse on his Union opponent at Fredericksburg.

Pres. Abraham Lincoln felt increasing pressure from abolitionists in the Republican Party, and he needed to weaken the Confederacy by encouraging enslaved African Americans to withhold their for the Confederate war effort. Lincoln subsequently published a notice stating that if the Southern states did not cease their attempt to form a separate nation by January 1, 1863, all slaves in the areas still in rebellion would be declared free. Given the Confederacy's military success during the summer and autumn of 1862, the South had little motive to accept this method of ending the war, even though doing so would have perpetuated slavery in the United States.

The events of December 1862 reinforced the Confederacy's disinclination to accept Lincoln's offer of terms on which to end the war. Following the Confederate move into Kentucky and the successful defense of the Union base

Abraham Lincoln.

at Corinth, Mississippi, Grant moved south through central Mississippi in an attempt to capture Vicksburg. Once Grant had drawn near enough to Vicksburg from the north and east to pin Confederate forces in place, Gen. William Sherman was to move down the Mississippi River and attack Vicksburg from that direction. This plan was frustrated when, on December 20, 1862, 1,700 Confederate cavalry led by Gen. Earl Van Dorn swept around the flank of the US advance and destroyed Grant's base of supply at Holly Springs, Mississippi. At the same time, Nathan Bedford Forrest was wreaking havoc on US supply lines in West Tennessee so that Grant could not replace the supplies Van Dorn had destroyed. Without Grant to attack from the east toward Vicksburg, Gen. William T. Sherman made a forlorn attack on Confederate defenses at Chickasaw Bluff, Mississippi, and suffered a stinging repulse.

While these events were taking place in Mississippi and West Tennessee, Gen. John Hunt Morgan led a force of two thousand cavalry on a raid that thoroughly wrecked the Louisville & Nashville Railroad, leaving Rosecrans's army without a dependable line of supply. On the last day of the year, Bragg led the Army of Tennessee in a successful attack that doubled Rosecrans's army back on itself. Only Rosecrans's stubborn persistence kept his force on the battlefield.

Had January 1, 1863, arrived with the news of Union defeats at Holly Springs, Chickasaw Bluffs, Fredericksburg, and Murfreesboro, and with the headlines of all newspapers reading, "Emancipation Proclamation Goes into Effect," Lincoln's administration might not have survived. The president would surely have faced serious challenges from antiwar Democrats. At the least, the Emancipation Proclamation could have been perceived to be a cruel joke, a promise that could not be kept.

The victory won under Rosecrans's leadership should have placed him in high regard in Washington, but this was not the case. Rather, Rosecrans faced problems he would have to resolve before he could make more progress against the Confederates. Some people, both in and out of the army, held a negative opinion of the general because of his religion. Rosecrans was a devout Roman Catholic who attended Mass as often as he could. At the time, anti-Catholic sentiment ran rather high since the Catholic Church was associated with Irish immigrants and other scorned groups. The Know-Nothing Party, with its anti-Catholic and anti-immigrant platform, had only recently ceased to exist, and anti-immigrant sentiment was still common.

Furthermore, questions arose about Rosecrans's political views. Some prominent Northern leaders wanted him to run for president and use his military reputation to challenge Lincoln, whose popularity was declining. Though Horace Greeley of the *New York Tribune* had originally backed Lincoln's nomination and election, he had lost confidence in the president. Twice Lincoln had mentioned resigning, and now Greeley was ready to help make that happen. The newspaperman saw Rosecrans as the only successful Union general. Therefore, he wanted Lincoln to resign and Vice President Hannibal Hamlin to appoint Rosecrans as commander of all Union armies. From this point the general's step to the presidency would be easy.

William S. Rosecrans.

The unresolved issue was Rosecrans's stand on slavery. Was he opposed to the institution? Rosecrans had already circulated a letter in several midwestern states making clear his support for the war. Therein he said, "This war is for the maintenance of the Constitution and the laws. I am amazed that anyone can think of peace on any terms. He who entertains the sentiment is fit only to be a slave; he who utters it is a traitor to his country." This statement was not clear enough for Secretary of War Edwin Stanton, who feared that Rosecrans planned to become the hero of the opposition and become president either by a coup or an election.

Seeking to resolve all doubts as to where the general stood on slavery, Greeley sent an old friend, James A. Gilmore, to visit Rosecrans. In a conversation that was later made public, Rosecrans told Gilmore, "The Negro should be given a Bible, a spelling book, freedom, and a chance for something more than six feet of ground. Then he should be left alone." Rosecrans cemented his stand on slavery by writing a letter to the editor of the *Catholic Telegraph* of Cincinnati: "[Congratulations on] the splendid stand you take against slavery. Slavery is dead." Greeley promptly republished this missive in the *New York Tribune.* This seemed a good, middle-of-the-road position on the slavery issue, one that would appeal to many voters. Rosecrans was opposed to slavery and favored an end to the institution, but he did not favor the Radicals' position of racial equality. However, the general put a period to the question of his presidential ambitions when he later told Gilmore that he was a soldier and would remain one.[1]

The fact that the major general commanding favored an end to slavery did not resolve the issue in the minds of many of his soldiers. Most of the men in the ranks of Rosecrans's command came from the Midwest. Although the area had always been one of "free states," the motive for keeping out slavery was economic rather than moral. Free labor, it was argued, should not have to compete with slave labor. Midwesterners also harbored antipathy against African Americans. None of the region's states recognized free African Americans as citizens or granted them equal rights. Indiana, Illinois, and Iowa had laws on the books designed to keep free people of color from settling in those states, and the Land Grant Act of 1863 denied free African Americans the opportunity to homestead land in the western territories.

Gen. David Stanley, commander of cavalry in the Army of the Cumberland, exemplified the complexity of this issue. Stanley did not like slaveholders, yet he was one. Though he recognized the evils of the slave system, he could not resist the opportunity to make life more comfortable for himself and his wife, so he hired three slaves and owned two more.[2]

In the Midwest, the Emancipation Proclamation was seen not as an attempt to rescue brothers from bondage but as an economic commodity—one of the sinews of war—to be denied the enemy. On April 28, 1863, the commander of the Department of the Ohio issued General Order No. 53 declaring it illegal to help any slave of a loyal man to escape or to prevent any loyal man from reclaiming his slaves. At the same time, the order deemed it illegal for anyone who was pro-Confederate to own or keep slaves.[3] This attitude of "pragmatic emancipation" became the approach adopted throughout Rosecrans's command. Consider the views of James Connolly of the 123rd Illinois. In a letter to his wife he proclaimed himself a conservative Democrat, yet he also stated, "While in the field I am an Abolitionist; my government has decided to wipe out slavery and I am for the government and its policy whether right or wrong."[4]

Both these issues, politics and emancipation, affected morale in Rosecrans's army. The commanding general spent a good deal of time and effort resolving the resulting difficulties. While dealing with these problems, Rosecrans was also contemplating the strategic situation and reaching critical decisions that would shape the Tullahoma Campaign and its aftermath.

Braxton Bragg had experienced a roller-coaster ride during 1862 himself. He had performed well at Pensacola, organizing and training troops, and the large command that he had led north to Corinth had fought well at Shiloh. Bragg's performance during the Union advance against Corinth had won him the confidence and respect of the War Department in Richmond. Thus when Gen. P. G. T. Beauregard took an unauthorized sick leave, Jefferson Davis appointed Bragg commander of the main Confederate army in the West.

Bragg had proven to have a sound grasp of strategy when he used the railroads to move his army from Mississippi to Chattanooga, Tennessee, and then to advance into Kentucky. In so doing, he had forced the Union armies in Tennessee to abandon much of their gains and concentrate against him. In contrast, Bragg had proven to be a poor tactician at Mumfordville. There, he had drawn aside and opened the route for Union forces to reach Louisville, allowing himself to be caught with his troops scattered over a wide area when Union general Buell concentrated against him at Perryville.

Public opinion began to question Bragg's capacity for command when the army, soon to be named the Army of Tennessee, had concentrated around Murfreesboro in November 1862. Bragg, however, had met with Davis, and the two agreed that Kentuckians had shown no inclination to offer large-scale support to the Confederacy, even though a number expressed sympathy for the Confederate cause. In its camps around Murfreesboro, the Army of Tennessee had maintained high morale and had improved in discipline and training.

The Battle of Stones River, called the Battle of Murfreesboro by the Confederates, reawakened the questions about Bragg's ability as a field commander. Bragg himself felt that he and his army had done well in the battle. He informed Joseph Johnston, his department commander, that his troops had extracted a large price from Rosecrans in return for the Union advance from Nashville to Murfreesboro. The Army of Tennessee still held major portions of Middle Tennessee and its abundant resources of food and horses. In addition, Bragg's men were ready to oppose any advance Rosecrans might make while harassing him every day if he did not move forward.

Bragg also pointed out that if he had not been ordered to send troops to Mississippi, he would have had a reserve of five thousand or more men with which to follow up his advantage won on the first day at Stones River.[5] General Johnston responded by enhancing Bragg's ability to gather food and to harass the enemy by ordering almost all Confederate cavalry in Mississippi to move to join Bragg's left flank at Spring Hill, Tennessee. Gen. Earl Van Dorn, fresh from his successful attack on Grant's supply base at Holly Springs, Mississippi, was placed in command with Bedford Forrest as his second-in-command. Joseph Wheeler commanded the cavalry on Bragg's right flank. This move gave Bragg the largest concentration of cavalry any general in North America had ever had under his command, about fourteen thousand troopers.

Bragg had thc confidcncc of his immcdiatc supcriors, but his subordi nates were another question. The manner in which he handled his relations

Earl Van Dorn.

Nathan Bedford Forrest.

with them would become one of the critical decisions of the Tullahoma Campaign and would affect later events as well.

Of necessity, Bragg spent a lot of time studying maps and contemplating the geography where he had taken position. While there were abundant food supplies in Middle Tennessee, he had to collect and ship them to his supply depot at Tullahoma. Col. Lucius Northrop, the Confederate commissary general, had ordered that all food supplies from the Sequatchie Valley, immediately to the rear of Bragg's headquarters at Tullahoma, and to the east were to be shipped to the Army of Northern Virginia. The Army of Tennessee was to supply itself from the country to its west, or left flank, and to its front. Bragg therefore had his supplies out front, his cavalry behind the supplies, and the infantry tying together the two wings of his cavalry. This very awkward position was not one of Bragg's creating.

Spring Hill, Tennessee, is only a short distance north of Columbia, and that town became the point at which supplies were connected. From Columbia it is about forty miles east by road to Tullahoma, but the 1863 roads were so wretched as to be almost unusable in the winter weather.

Bragg repaired the Nashville & Decatur Railroad south to the Tennessee River. There, supplies were switched onto the Memphis & Charleston Railroad east to Stevenson, Alabama, and then switched north on the Nashville & Chattanooga Railroad to Tullahoma. Some supplies were loaded on steamboats for the journey from Decatur to Stevenson and then sent onward by rail.[6]

This lengthy rail route made the amassing of supplies difficult, and the whole network was vulnerable to cavalry raids by Union horsemen. As a result, the Army of Tennessee seldom had more than a few days' supply of food in its warehouses. Drawing food from the western part of Middle Tennessee meant that Bragg had to position his army to the southwest of the most direct line of advance from Murfreesboro to Chattanooga. His position was then liable to being outflanked to the east.

As Bragg sat in his headquarters, the home of US Supreme Court associate justice John Catron,[7] he must have thought, "What a lot of roads." A veritable spider's web of roads radiated out from Murfreesboro, and Rosecrans was the spider sitting at the center of the web, free to move along any strand. Bragg was the fly, buzzing around the circumference of the web, always keeping an eye on the spider.

On the western end of Bragg's line, a good road led south from Franklin to his cavalry base at Spring Hill. Franklin was in Union hands and was connected to both Nashville and Murfreesboro. This corridor gave Union and Confederate troops a way to move north and south against each other, and control of this route would be crucial as the Tullahoma Campaign developed. Another road leading south into Confederate territory intersected the Franklin–Murfreesboro road at Triuine and provided access to Shelbyville, the anchor of Bragg's left infantry flank. From Murfreesboro one route led south to Shelbyville via Guy's Gap, while another branched off from it at Christiana to lead to Bell Buckle via Liberty Gap. Running east-southeast from Murfreesboro was the Manchester Pike that ascended the Highland Rim at Hoover's Gap and gave access to Bragg's right flank. Another road led due east from Murfreesboro to Pocahontas, where it turned southeast to reach Manchester, again providing access to Bragg's right flank. This last route was the best one, and it was the road most often used for travel from Murfreesboro to Chattanooga.

In addition, the Nashville & Chattanooga Railroad ran southeast and then east from Murfreesboro, passing through Bell Buckle and Tullahoma. It then crossed the Elk River on its way to Stevenson, Alabama, and a junction with the Memphis & Charleston Railroad. The length of line Bragg was forced to maintain to cover all these approaches to his position would ultimately influence some of the critical decisions he made as the Tullahoma Campaign developed.

In response to the geography confronting him, Bragg placed his cavalry on each wing of his army. Van Dorn was stationed at Spring Hill, and Wheeler established John Hunt Morgan at McMinnville. Hardee's infantry corps went into winter quarters at Tullahoma, while Polk's Corps did the same at Shelbyville. Bragg was forced to cover some seventy-five miles of front with fourteen thousand cavalry and thirty-two thousand infantry.

Attempting to improve his manpower situation, Bragg appointed Gen. Gideon Pillow to head his Conscript Bureau. Pillow remained a popular political figure in Tennessee despite his performance at Fort Donelson. He filled his new role well, bringing Bragg some 10,000 recruits during the 6 months between the Battle of Stones River and the beginning of the Tullahoma Campaign. The problem was training and arming the soldiers. Bragg reported only 64 pieces of artillery in his army in January, but he increased this supply to 125 pieces by May. However, 80 of this number were obsolescent 6-pounders and 12-pounder howitzers, while another 16 were 12-pounder Napoleons. Bragg had only 29 rifled pieces.[8] Only 20,000 of the approximately 32,000 infantry in Bragg's army had rifles; the rest carried smoothbores. Only 1,500 of the cavalry had carbines, while 4,700 had long-barreled rifles. Some 753 cavalrymen carried shotguns they had brought from home. Only 1,566 of the cavalrymen reported having a revolver, though some had single-shot pistols. The weak armament of the Army of Tennessee would be a factor in the coming campaign.[9]

As each army commander pondered what would prove to be critical decisions, tactical events influenced the development of the Tullahoma

Joseph Wheeler.

Campaign. The first of these involved attempts by Confederate cavalry forces to interrupt the flow of supplies from Louisville to Nashville via the Cumberland River. As John Hunt Morgan's December raid had put the Louisville & Nashville Railroad out of service, Rosecrans was heavily dependent on riverboats to supply his army. On January 8, 1863, Gen. Joseph Wheeler led a raid to the outskirts of Nashville and then followed the Cumberland River west and northwest to Clarksville. Dividing his force into two groups, Wheeler blockaded the river for several days, capturing several boats and preventing supplies from reaching Rosecrans for a week.[10]

Seeking to reinforce this success, Wheeler, seconded by Nathan Bedford Forrest, was ordered to move against the river traffic again on February 2. Wheeler decided to attack a Union garrison at Dover, Tennessee, the site of Fort Donelson. The garrison did not occupy any of the fortifications that had been captured by General Grant in February 1862 but were entrenched in the middle of the village of Dover. Confederates repulsed an assault on the Union works but suffered significant losses. As the battered Southern cavalry fell back toward Spring Hill, Forrest confronted Wheeler and informed him he would never again consent to serve under his command. This breach in relations between the two would present Rosecrans with an opportunity that he could exploit via a critical decision several months later.[11]

Following this contretemps, Wheeler was given command of cavalry on Bragg's right flank. Earl Van Dorn, who had just arrived from Mississippi, was placed in command on Bragg's left with Forrest as his subordinate. On

March 4 the Confederates encountered a Union force including an infantry brigade, two cavalry regiments, and an artillery battery advancing south from Franklin toward Spring Hill. On March 5 Van Dorn led his command into battle with this expedition, which was commanded by Col. John Coburn, near Thompson's Station. Van Dorn had the advantage of numbers and position, and Coburn found himself outflanked, especially on his left, where Forrest had led his brigade in a sweeping flanking movement. Despite the firepower provided by his infantry, Coburn found himself overrun and was forced to surrender. His losses totaled about 400 dead and wounded and 1,300 captured out of a total force of 2,837.[12]

The Confederates struck again on March 24, attacking and capturing a depot of supplies at Brentwood and breaking up a bridge on the Hapeth River. In April, Van Dorn continued to operate against the Union cavalry in the Franklin sector of the lines, while Forrest was detached to pursue Col. Abel Streight's Union force attempting to sever the rail line at Rome, Georgia. This line brought no food to the Army of Tennessee but was the source of ordnance supplies. The pursuit and capture of Streight's entire command became one of the fabled exploits of the Forrest and his men.[13]

Upon returning from his pursuit of Streight on May 16, Forrest found that General Van Dorn had been shot and killed by a jealous husband. Forrest was now in command of the cavalry on the Confederate left—two divisions. The division led by William Hicks "Red" Jackson was transferred back to

Abel Streight.

Mississippi within days, and Forrest was wounded in a confrontation with Lieut. Wills Gould, an artilleryman he planned to transfer out of his command for dissatisfactory service, within a month. Forrest only suffered a flesh wound, but its location and susceptibility to infection kept him from exercising field command at the crucial period when the Tullahoma Campaign opened.[14]

While success was elusive for the Union cavalry facing Van Dorn and Forrest, another story was developing on the Confederate right flank. Gen. John Hunt Morgan commanded a cavalry line stretching over one hundred miles from Woodbury, Tennessee, to Monticello, Kentucky. Morgan spent most of his time at his headquarters in McMinnville, Tennessee, where he was accompanied by his new bride, Matty. His men felt neglected by their commander, and their discipline began to slip. On March 18 Rosecrans sent a mixed force of infantry and cavalry to probe the area Morgan held. The Union's progress halted at the village of Milton when Morgan advanced, with the US troops taking position on a steep hill. Without reconnaissance, Morgan ordered his dismounted cavalrymen on a series of frontal attacks. After only an hour of furious and costly assaults, the Southern soldiers ran out of ammunition and had to retreat. Morgan obviously had not paid attention to the provisioning of his men.

On April 1 Morgan faced another Union advance at Snow Hill. Although the Confederates held a strong defensive position that should have been maintained easily, the men fought with little determination and fell back when the pressure began to build against their lines. Morgan himself failed

John Hunt Morgan.

to rally his men—they calmly and deliberately rode off the field. Just over two weeks later, on April 19, Gen. J. J. Reynolds, accompanied by John Wilder's brigade of mounted infantry, overran inattentive Confederate pickets and swept into McMinnville, scattering the garrison there and coming within a hairsbreadth of capturing Morgan himself.[15]

Tactically, the numerous cavalry encounters on the Confederate left did not affect the course of events. But the results of these encounters provided Rosecrans with information he used to reach some critical decisions. Circumstances such as the wounding of Forrest and the disintegration of morale and combat effectiveness of Morgan's command would play an important role in reaching decisions affecting the coming campaign.

While these events were playing out, Bragg was dealing with some personal problems. His poor health during the winter months of early 1863 seemed to sap his physical and mental energy. Bragg developed no plan of defense, no strategy for a response to the move Rosecrans was certain to make sooner or later. Illness and lack of planning contributed to deteriorating relationships between Bragg and many of his subordinate officers, especially Hardee. When active campaigning began in late June, the Union thrust was directed at Hardee's sector of the line, and Hardee was slow to inform Bragg of what was happening. This lack of communication and absence of a plan for cooperation had disastrous consequences for the Army of Tennessee.

The feuding between Bragg and his subordinate officers negatively impacted the Army of Tennessee's performance during the Tullahoma Campaign. However, the decision to engage in these squabbles was made before the Tullahoma Campaign began and continued after it had ended. Although these personal relations affected the campaign, they do not constitute a critical decision made during the campaign.

Six months passed following the Battle of Stones River and the opening of the Tullahoma Campaign. During this time both commanding generals made numerous decisions that seemed routine and took many actions necessary for running an army. They also made some critical decisions. In many cases, no clear line can be drawn between the routine and the critical decisions because events that seemed commonplace at their occurrence took on added significance with the passing of time. But on June 22, 1863, action began in the Tullahoma Campaign. The next ten days would be some of the most momentous of the entire Civil War.

On the eve of the active phase of the Tullahoma Campaign, the Army of Tennessee was in relatively good condition so far as manpower, weapons, and supplies were concerned. The addition of recruits and the return of convalescents had swelled the ranks, all soldiers had weapons, and food was adequate though not abundant. The greatest problem the Tennessee army faced was the disintegration of its command structure.

The Army of the Cumberland had increased its numbers since the fighting at Murfreesboro, and many of these added men had some prior military experience. Rosecrans had successfully drawn on the factories and arsenals to arm his men with a sufficient number of the best weapons available. The construction of Fortress Rosecrans and the filling of its warehouses meant the army would have a secure base with an adequate supply reserve. The Army of the Cumberland faced the logistics problem of covering the distance from Murfreesboro to its front line by traveling over poor roads. Union forces' strongest feature was their well-organized command structure comprised of men who were willing to cooperate for the success of their commander.

The Tullahoma Campaign is a unique occurrence in Civil War history. The purpose of the campaign was not to bring the opponent to battle but to avoid battle and achieve victory by maneuvering the enemy out of position. Rosecrans achieved this goal in an exemplary fashion. He shed the sweat of his men but not their blood. Instead of having his soldiers endure the test of combat, he endured the tedium of scouting, reconnaissance, and intelligence gathering. Finally, he allowed his reputation and standing with his superiors in Washington to be wounded in order to save the bodies of his men. This severe test of leadership and of character was also an excellent example of military planning. Critical decisions were not made amid the smoke and noise of battle but were reached by deliberate thought and discussion over a period of months.

Little combat occurred once the active phase of the campaign began. At most, the infantry engagements at Liberty Gap and Hoover's Gap involved two brigades on the Confederate side and a division on the Union side. Neither of these engagements resulted in prolonged combat, although skirmishing lasted for three days at each location. Many of the soldiers engaged in the Tullahoma Campaign never fired their weapons except to clear them of rounds dampened by the incessant rain.

Ironically, Rosecrans's careful planning and successful maneuvering cost him the fame and attention his victory should have earned. Public attention was drawn to the copious bloodshed at Gettysburg and the mass surrender at Vicksburg so that the achievements of the Tullahoma Campaign were not recognized or celebrated. Rosecrans protested that what the Army of the Cumberland had done should not be overlooked because it was "not writ large in letters of blood," but that is precisely what has happened.

CHAPTER 1

BEFORE THE CAMPAIGN

The criteria for determining a critical decision are discussed in the preface. Please keep those criteria in mind while reading the discussion of what these decisions were and how they affected the Tullahoma Campaign. The introduction has set the stage for the discussion of critical decisions by providing general background for the events that transpired between the end of the Battle of Stones River and the beginning of active campaigning in the Tullahoma Campaign.

Bragg Holds the Line of the Duck River

Situation

On January 3, 1863, the battlefield situation at Murfreesboro was a stalemate. Neither side held a decided advantage, and both armies had taken serious losses. However, Braxton Bragg received false intelligence that Union reinforcements were approaching his right flank via the Lebanon Pike. The threat of enemy reinforcements, coupled with the advice of his corps commanders, Lieut. Gens. Leonidas Polk and William Hardee, convinced Bragg to back away from his opponent, Maj. Gen. William Rosecrans. Bragg then sought a defensive position that would allow the Confederates to hold on to as much of Middle Tennessee as they could. The region was important for food production, and it was also a major breeding area for horses, mules, and hogs. Moreover, it contained several manufacturing sites that produced iron, cloth, and gunpowder, and its considerable population could produce an important supply of recruits.

Iron City, Tennessee, was part of an area producing some seven hundred tons of pig iron annually. The pig iron–producing area was linked by water to Florence, Alabama, from which town the iron could be moved by rail to

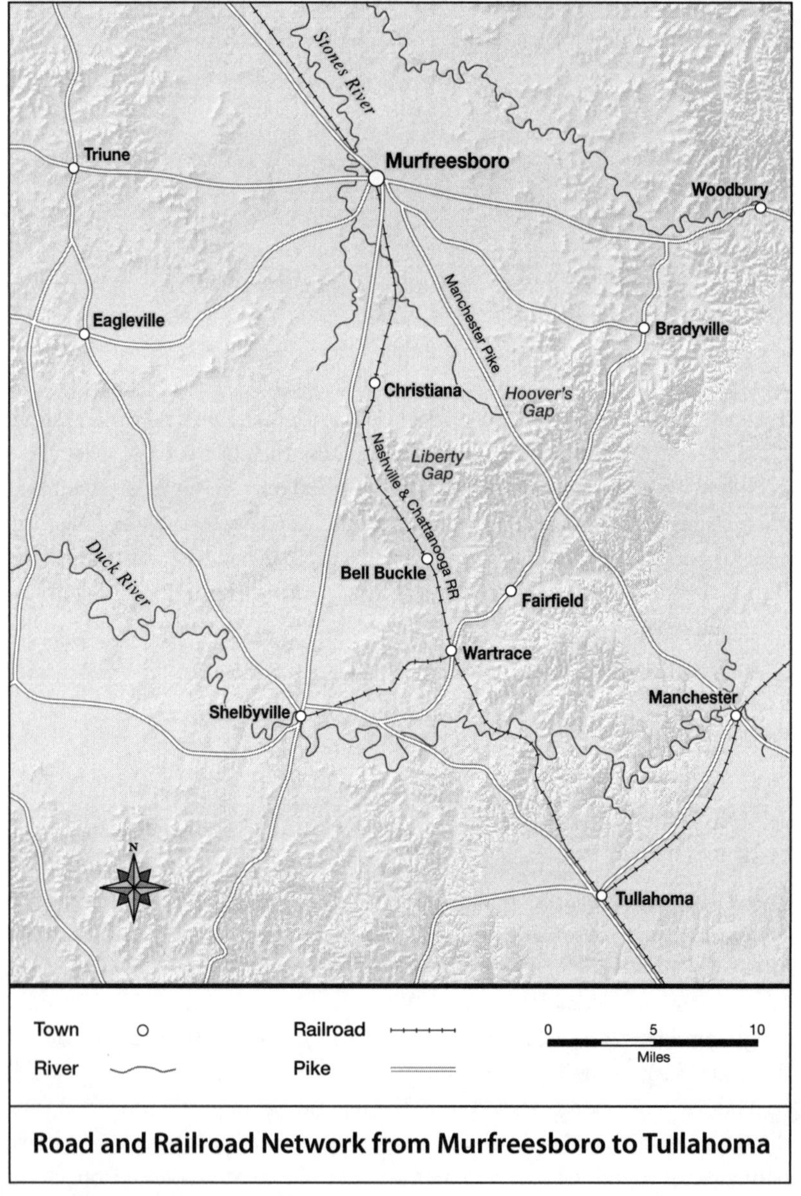

Road and Railroad Network from Murfreesboro to Tullahoma

Columbus, Augusta, and Macon, Georgia, where it was converted into ammunition or refined into steel. Lawrenceburg, Tennessee, had mills producing six thousand yards of cloth monthly for uniforms. Manchester, Tennessee, was the site of a gunpowder mill that furnished the Confederate armies 1,500 pounds of powder a week. Large mills for grinding cornmeal and flour were found on the Elk River and at Florence, Alabama.[1]

Two lines of defense offered themselves to Bragg—the line of Elk River, a stream rising at the foot of the Cumberland Plateau and running west and southwest into Alabama, or the line of Duck River and the Highland Rim. The Duck River rises somewhat farther west than the Elk but flows more westerly, joining the Tennessee River far to the west of Bragg's position. The Duck would cover the left flank of any potential Confederate line, while the center and right flank would be protected by the Highland Rim.

Nashville and Murfreesboro are located in the Cumberland Basin of Middle Tennessee. As one moves east, south, or west from these towns, one reaches a rugged line of hills ascending from eight hundred to one thousand feet above the basin. This line of hills is called the Highland Rim. In 1863 the a limited number of roads traversed the rim, all of them utilizing gaps in the hills to make the ascent.

Options

Bragg had three options available to him: He could hold the line of the Elk River farther east and south, or he could hold the line of the Duck River / Highland Rim farther west. A third choice would involve occupying the Duck River / Highland Rim line and using it as a base for offensive operations instead of holding a line for defensive purposes.

Option One

Bragg could occupy the line of the Elk River. Doing so would have protected the Nashville & Chattanooga Railroad, which brought the army most of its ordnance supplies. This option would also provide the army a secure line of retreat in case of need. Cavalry could protect the flanks; the river could protect the left of the army, and the rugged country to the north and west could prevent the right flank from being turned. The choice of this position would allow Bragg to block an important road leading from Murfreesboro to Chattanooga via Woodbury and McMinnville. However, this position would have made it difficult, if not impossible, for Bragg to utilize the area around Columbia, Tennessee, from which he was to provision his army.

Col. Lucius Northrop, the Confederate commissary general, had ordered the Army of Tennessee to gather food from an area to the west and southwest of its position. All foodstuffs from immediately behind Bragg's men through Georgia were reserved for the Army of Northern Virginia, and this created an awkward situation for Bragg. The area produced sufficient food to feed his army. However, the transportation net was poor and thus prevented a surplus of food from being collected. The food-producing area was also susceptible to cavalry raids by Union forces, and protecting it would also require placing the bulk of Confederate cavalry in that area.[2]

Option Two

Bragg could occupy the line of the Duck River / Highland Rim. This option would place Bragg closer to Rosecrans's force at Murfreesboro and would allow him to control more of Middle Tennessee and its valuable resources. Being closer to Murfreesboro would allow Bragg's cavalry to constantly observe and harass the Union forces occupying that area, thus hampering Rosecrans's planning of his next move.

The problem with this option was that the line was not compact. It would need to stretch for a distance of about seventy-five miles to cover the food-producing area and the road that ran from Murfreesboro to Chattanooga via McMinnville. Bragg did not have enough men to staff this line thoroughly.

Option Three

Finally, Bragg could occupy the line of the Duck River / Highland Rim and adopt an offensive strategy that kept Confederate cavalry constantly on the attack around Murfreesboro and between Nashville and Murfreesboro. As the Louisville & Nashville Railroad was repaired, the area of offensive operations could be extended into Kentucky to slow the reconstruction of the line and then to hamper its use.

Decision

Bragg opted to hold the line of the Duck River / Highland Rim as a defensive position. He deemed this choice necessary for two reasons. First, controlling as much of Middle Tennessee as possible was a valid objective. In addition, Bragg's decision obeyed Commissary General Northrup's orders to gather supplies for the army from the area around Columbia, Tennessee, and west (see note 2 of this chapter).

Results/Impact

Army headquarters was placed at Tullahoma, a convenient location because of its rail connections with McMinnville and Shelbyville. The railroad was paralleled by telegraph wires, so Bragg had good communication with the forward elements of his command as well as with Richmond.

Bragg placed his largest cavalry force in Columbia, Tennessee, to protect the left flank of the Confederate position and to guard the area from which food was to be gathered. Maj. Gen. Earl Van Dorn led these cavalrymen, and they oversaw the repair of the Nashville & Decatur Railroad leading south from Columbia to the Tennessee River at Decatur, Alabama. From that point, supplies for the army were switched to the Memphis & Charleston Railroad running east through Huntsville, Alabama, to Bridgeport. At Bridgeport, the Memphis & Charleston met the Nashville & Chattanooga Railroad leading back to Tullahoma. Riverboats that carried goods from Decatur to Bridgeport supplemented this rail link. This patched-together supply line did not produce an abundance of food in the warehouses at Tullahoma, but neither did the army starve. Lincoln County alone produced eight hundred thousand pounds of salt pork for the army while still leaving plenty to feed the civilian population. The farmlands around Huntsville, Alabama, produced several hundred tons of corn that was ground into meal. Vegetables and flour were not in abundance, but pork and corn pone kept bellies full.[3]

Joseph Wheeler assumed charge of the cavalry on the right flank of the army, and his largest command was the brigade of John Hunt Morgan. Wheeler was notorious for not filing written reports, so much of his activity during this period is conjecture. Morgan had married Mattie Ready, a young woman half his age, in December 1862, and he spent a great deal of time in her company at his comfortable headquarters at McMinnville. With both commanders inactive, the condition and morale of the men suffered. Bragg did not intervene to correct this situation.

The deteriorating confidence and effectiveness of the cavalry on the Confederate right flank would decidedly impact the direction of the campaign. These conditions influenced Rosecrans to direct his primary move toward these troops. For his part, Hardee placed his corps in winter quarters at Tullahoma with forward positions at Wartrace, Bell Buckle, and Hoover's Gap. Polk positioned his men at Shelbyville, which he fortified heavily, with outposts at Rover and Guy's Gap. Finally, with the exception of the cavalry under Van Dorn, the Confederate forces adopted a defensive attitude and waited for Rosecrans to make the next move.

Alternative Scenerio

Bragg might have recognized that Rosecrans could be defeated by emulating the Lilliputians' treatment of Gulliver in the story *Gulliver's Travels*—in other words, by tying Rosecrans down with threads. This could have been done by keeping all Confederate cavalry constantly on the offensive, forcing the Union army to stay close to the environs of Murfreesboro, constantly raiding the Louisville & Nashville Railroad, and attacking forage parties at every opportunity. Bragg would have had to pay close attention to the physical condition and morale of his cavalry. In addition, he would have had to promote cooperation among Van Dorn, Forrest, Wheeler, and Morgan. Successful offensive operations would have built the troops' confidence and eased friction between the commanders while encouraging Morgan and Wheeler to remain attentive to their soldiers.

In making constant hit-and-run attacks on Union lines and foraging parties, Confederate cavalry at the edge of Murfreesboro would probably have challenged the ability of the limited cavalry forces of the Army of the Cumberland. Furthermore, these forces might have exacerbated the morale problem related to emancipation. It is possible that the constant irritation such tactics produced would have worked on the anxious personality of Rosecrans, which later led to his nervous breakdown following Chickamauga. The annoyance of ongoing attacks could have disrupted his relations with Washington, leading to a change of leadership for the Army of the Cumberland or to a failed attempt to attack the Confederate position.

A policy of offense, instead of defense, might have provided a different conclusion for the Tullahoma Campaign.

Rosecrans Secures His Line of Supply

Situation

In December 1862, prior to Rosecrans's advance to Murfreesboro, a Confederate cavalry raid led by John Hunt Morgan had briefly occupied the town of Gallatin, Tennessee. Just outside that town the Louisville & Nashville Railroad passed through the so-called twin tunnels in adjacent hills. Seams of coal ran through the hills, and Morgan destroyed the tunnels by running strings of empty boxcars into each of them and setting the cars afire. The flames spread to the coal seams, bringing down the roofs of the tunnels and rendering the L&N inoperable for several months. During Morgan's subsequent Christmas Raid, he destroyed the nine hundred feet of trestles at Muldraughs Hill, Kentucky, further delaying the time at which the rails would serve as a line of supply for the Union forces in Middle Tennessee. While wagons bridged the gaps in the railroad, this slow transportation method did not furnish the quantity of supplies necessary for the army's forward movement.[4]

Although left in possession of the field at Stones River, Rosecrans found himself with no railroad to supply his army. The general commanding then

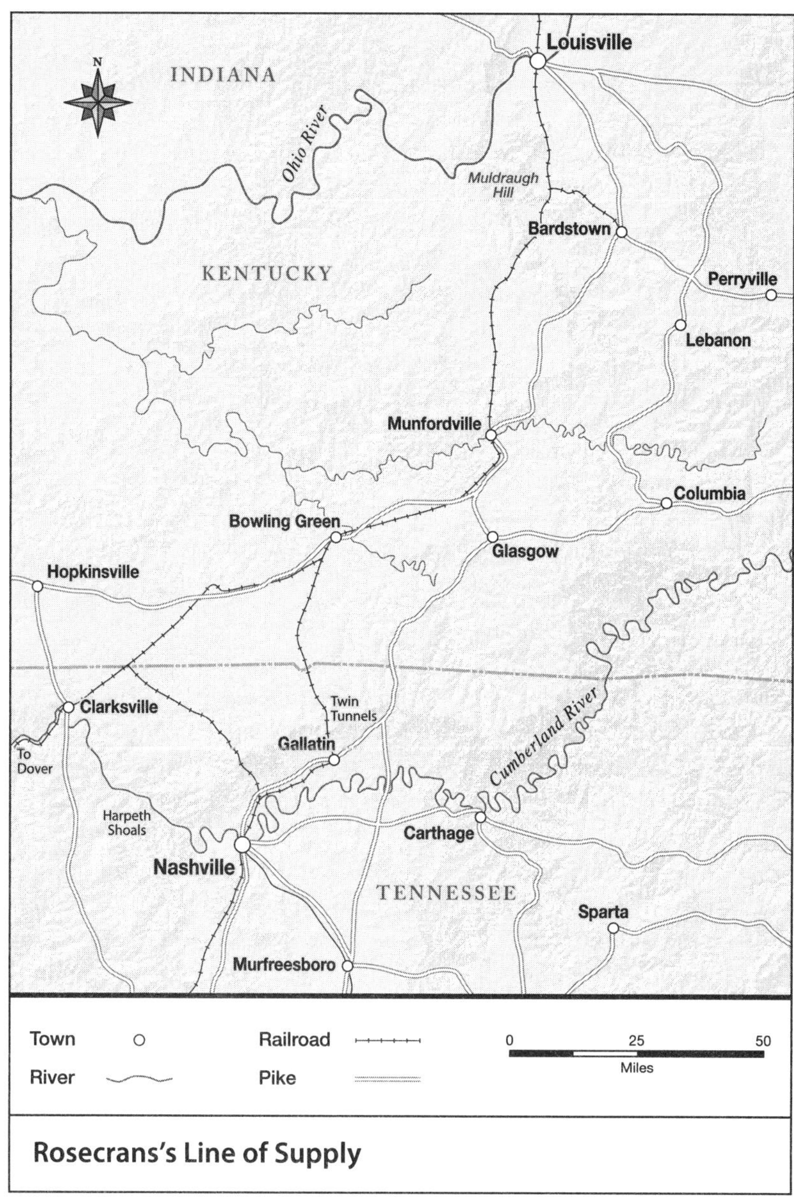

Rosecrans's Line of Supply

looked to a secondary route, the Cumberland River. Boats from Louisville, Cincinnati, Saint Louis, and even Pittsburg could reach Nashville by traveling the Ohio, Mississippi, and Cumberland Rivers. However, the winter of 1862–63 was unusually dry, and the level of water in the river did not rise as usual. This meant that boats had to pass upstream through narrow channels while battling swift water. At places the current was so strong that a boat bound upstream could travel at only one mile per hour. The sites of these swift currents became choke points that roving regiments of Confederate cavalry could readily block with a couple of fieldpieces. Even guerrillas blocked the passage of boats on occasion.

Nashville held enough supplies for a short campaign if Rosecrans wished to pursue Bragg, but the depot there could only be replenished slowly. Moreover, the weather was uncertain. Rosecrans wrote the following to the War Department: "Our lines of communication and our depots absorb much force, and that increases as we advance. . . . The country is full of natural passes and fortifications and demands superior force to advance with any success."[5]

Options

Rosecrans had two options. He could lead his army on a brief foray forward to press the Confederates back a short distance farther, or he could consolidate his line of supplies in preparation for a more decisive move.

Option One

Rosecrans had limited supplies but a short advance following Bragg was possible. At the moment, Rosecrans was the hero of the hour. He had won the only clear Union victory since Shiloh, and his success at Stones River had saved the Lincoln administration much embarrassment relative to military success and the Emancipation Proclamation. Lincoln declared to the general, "I can never forget, whilst I remember anything, that about the end of last year and the beginning of this, you gave us a hard-earned victory, which, had there been a defeat instead, the nation could hardly have lived." An advance of fewer than twenty miles would allow Rosecrans to occupy one or more of the gaps leading up onto the Highland Rim, rendering Bragg's position untenable.[6]

This option entailed several dangers, among them the weather. Winter in Middle Tennessee is typically chilly and wet with occasional short periods of intense cold. Rain, followed by freezing and thawing, could render the roads impassable so that an attempted advance risked literally bogging down in the mud. This, of course, happened at about this very time in Virginia when Burnside led the Army of the Potomac on its infamous Mud March.

Option Two

Rosecrans could put his army in winter quarters around Murfreesboro and take the time needed to rebuild the rail net supplying his men. At the same time, he could create a safe base of operations for further moves.

While Rosecrans was receiving telegrams of congratulations from prominent persons all over the North, he knew the War Department had limited patience with delay and lack of aggressive action. These were the very qualities that had cost Rosecrans's predecessor his position. Waiting could be fatal to a career.

Decision

Rosecrans chose to secure his line of supplies in preparation for a more decisive move later in the year. To carry out this decision, Rosecrans accepted a lengthy delay by placing his army in winter quarters while constructing a secure depot and repairing the rail line leading to it from Louisville, Kentucky.

This decision affected the Tullahoma Campaign in a major way; the decision delayed any movement by the Army of the Cumberland for several months and allowed the Army of Tennessee time to recover and prepare to receive Rosecrans's next move. This delay also eroded the goodwill between Rosecrans and the War Department that existed at the end of the Stones River Campaign. Events would prove this decision both prudent and effective.

Results/Impact

The most obvious result of Rosecrans's decision was the construction of the largest earthwork fortification ever built on the North American continent. The chief engineer of the Army of the Cumberland, Brig. James S. Morton, was given the task of designing a fortification to protect a supply base large enough to allow the army to advance. General Morton chose a site covering over two hundred acres on the western side of Murfreesboro. The land belonged to the Maney and Lytle families, both prominent secessionists, so it was confiscated. Morton designed an earthen fortification running 1,250 yards north to south and 1,070 yards east to west. The circumference of the fort would total more than two miles, and its outer wall consisted of lunettes, earthworks shaped something like an arrowhead. The lunettes were spaced a few hundred yards apart but connected by curtain walls, or breast-high mounds of dirt behind which infantry could take cover. Each lunette would hold field artillery positioned to fire parallel to the curtain walls. Outside the walls was a ditch six feet wide and six feet deep. All timber, brush, and high grass was cut or burned for a distance of 1,450 yards to clear a field of fire.

Inside the outer line was a series of four rectangular redoubts in which large-caliber artillery was mounted. Some of these guns had a bore eight inches in diameter, while others fired shells weighing sixty-four pounds. Each of these redoubts was designed to stand alone should the outer curtain wall be breached

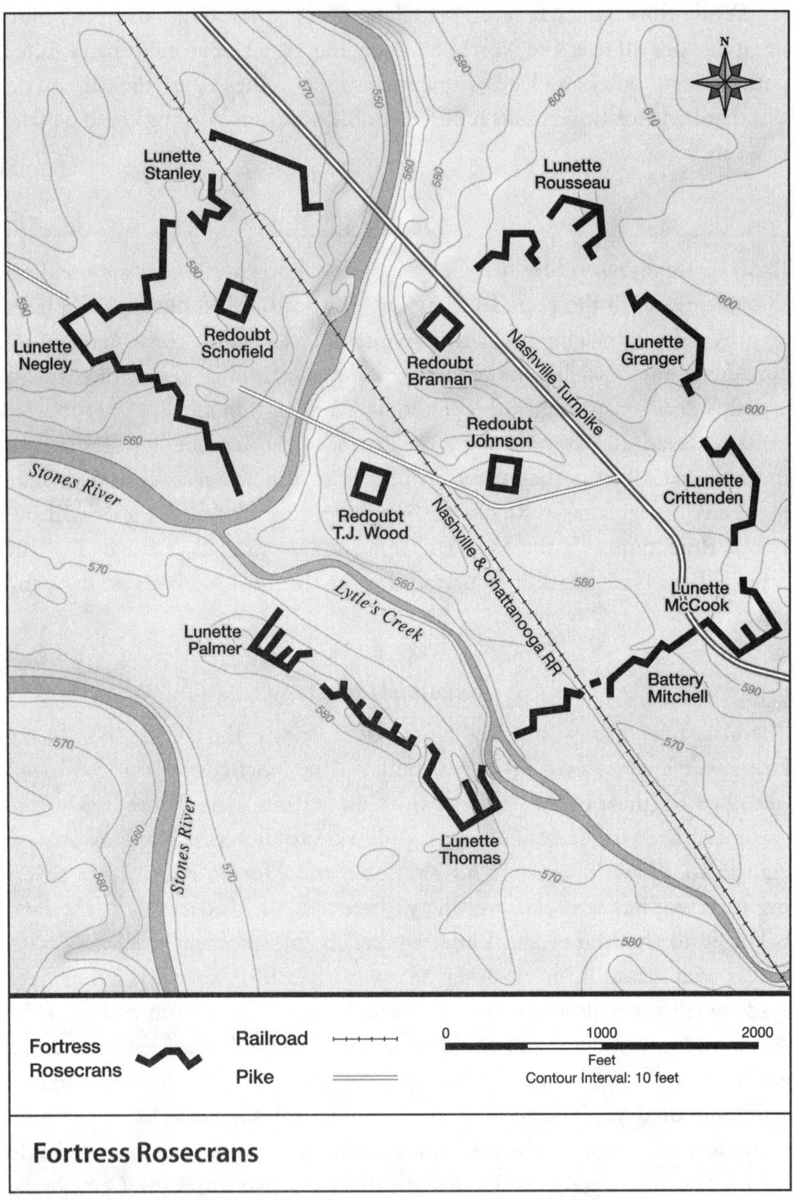

Fortress Rosecrans

or even should one of the other redoubts be captured. Five demilunes, or semicircular earthworks, also stood outside the curtain walls to protect the railroad as it entered the fort at the north and south side. Another demilune was built to protect the Nashville Pike.[7]

Work began on the fortifications on January 23, 1863, with labor performed by rotating details from each infantry unit and hundreds of hired African American men. Construction went on twenty-four hours a day, seven days a week, and it involved up to seven thousand men at any given time. Murfreesboro resident John Spence kept a diary during the war years in which he noted, "Large numbers of timber trees are cut and hauled to the grounds. The work is commenced and pushed on vigorously—digging and blasting rocks. A great number of Negros are employed at this kind of work, under pay, of course."[8]

The fortification was not merely for defense; it was intended to be the main army base and supply depot for the forward movement of the Union forces in Middle Tennessee. As such, it was designed to house fifty thousand men with enough supplies to last ninety days. Inside the walls were three commissary depots, a quartermaster depot, two ordnance depots, an engineering depot, an artillery depot, and four sawmills. The tracks of the Nashville & Chattanooga passed through the fortification, so loading and unloading railcars could be done in a secure location. By mid-February supplies were reaching Nashville by river, but only fifteen days of surplus food was in Murfreesboro.[9]

By March 1863 the works were complete enough that the camps of several units moved inside the walls. The fortification was named for the general commanding, being known as Fortress Rosecrans.

Once a secure line of supply had been anchored in a protected depot, Rosecrans could turn his attention to addressing other pressing matters.

Alternative Scenario

Rosecrans faced the necessity of making sure supplies reached his army. By late February provisions were trickling into Nashville, and a limited forward move was conceivable. The vulnerable area from which the Army of Tennessee drew its supplies offered Rosecrans a viable strategic target. The road from Franklin, Tennessee, to Columbia was a good one and was usable in all weather. Securely in Union hands, Franklin was fortified as a forward post.

Rosecrans might have concentrated infantry to support his cavalry and made a foray south from Franklin with the intention of capturing Columbia. Brig. Gen. Grenville Dodge, commanding Union forces at Corinth, could have pushed toward Florence, Alabama, to threaten Columbia from the southwest. If successful, this combined move would have forced Bragg to draw supplies from Atlanta, further complicating his logistical situation. Though amove on Columbia would not have forced a Confederate retreat from Middle Tennessee, it held the possibility of worsening the Rebels' position and thus strengthening that of Rosecrans.

Rosecrans Strengthens His Cavalry

Situation

The cavalry under Rosecrans's command were outnumbered, outorganized, and outclassed. The Confederates had mustered over fourteen thousand cavalry in Middle Tennessee, while Rosecrans could bring less than a quarter of that number into the field. Much earlier in the conflict the Confederate War Department had authorized the organization of brigades and divisions of cavalry, thereby centralizing command and control. As Washington was slower to adopt this structure, the South had better organization. Leadership in Confederate ranks included such luminaries as Forrest and Wheeler, their seconds Van Dorn and Morgan, and a number of highly competent lower-ranking officers. Command of the cavalry in the Army of the Cumberland was feeble. Only two brigade commanders, Cols. Robert Minty and Eli Long, were competent. Col. Edward McCook was viewed as unstable, and two infantry officers assigned to duty with the cavalry, Brig. Gen. Robert T. Mitchell and Maj. Gen. John B. Turchin, proved to be disappointments. Morale was low among the cavalrymen, and Rosecrans's Fifteenth Pennsylvania was on the verge of mutiny. Fifteen of the regiment's men were court-martialed before the unit was restored to good order.[10]

On January 14, 1863, Confederate cavalry successfully attacked three riverboats downstream from Nashville, and two weeks later the troops captured a foraging train of thirty-four wagons and 164 men. The loss of the wagons was particularly grave. During the Stones River fighting, Confederate cavalry had destroyed about three hundred wagons belonging to the Army of the Cumberland, and the army could not afford to continue losing them. Without wagons the entire process of supplying the men would come to a halt. Rosecrans knew he could neither gather the intelligence needed for an advance nor collect necessary supplies without better horsemen.

While many contemporary historians contend that the almost-daily cavalry fights in the winter and spring of 1863 did not affect the military situation, Rosecrans's thinking indicates a different conclusion should be reached. Cavalry combat in early 1863 convinced the general that he could not advance and launch a successful campaign without strengthening his horsemen.

Improving the mounted arm could not be done quickly. It was generally agreed that recruits had to train for at least a year to be good cavalrymen. Rosecrans had no time for this instruction, and General Grant had no cavalry to spare. Had Grant had been willing to send cavalrymen to his rival, the quality of his own troops was no better than, if as good as, those already under Rosecrans's command. The Army of the Potomac was also clamoring for more and better cavalry, so Rosecrans could not expect any troopers to be transferred from that department.

Attempting to better conditions so his cavalry would not be called on so frequently, Rosecrans continued the program of fortification he had begun at Murfreesboro. He built blockhouses and small redoubts to protect bridges and water tanks on the railroad, and he called in all horses used in noncombat roles to mount more of his cavalrymen. Reorganizing his cavalry by placing brigades into divisions and increasing centralized control gained Rosecrans additional strength.[11]

The question of horses was of paramount importance. Both armies had been collecting mounts from Middle Tennessee since the spring of 1862, and the supply of animals suited for cavalry service was running low. Absent a local supply, Rosecrans began to requisition horses from the War Department, asking for twelve thousand animals immediately. Much to his disgust, he received a great many horses unfit for service due to age or illness. Over the first four months of 1863 Rosecrans received just over thirty-three thousand animals, including draft animals, of which he returned nine thousand as unfit. This constant bombardment of Quartermaster General Meigs and the War Department soon had Rosecrans losing favor in Washington. But the general still did not have enough horses to increase the size of his cavalry.[12]

Options

Rosecrans faced a knotty choice in dealing with his need for better cavalry. He could make do with his current level of efficiency and attempt to plan a campaign that minimized the role of mounted troops. Alternatively, he could face the ire of the War Department by delaying his next move until he had trained cavalry, although this choice might well cost him his job. Finally, Rosecrans could seek an innovative solution to make his cavalry stronger.

Option One

Rosecrans could follow General Grant's example and proceed with mediocre cavalry, both leaders and men, while developing a campaign that did not depend on the use of horsemen. The Vicksburg Campaign would be notable for the way Grant did not rely on cavalry.[13]

Option Two

Rosecrans could take the time needed to train cavalrymen. This slow process would certainly raise the ire of the War Department. Additionally, the delay caused by securing his supply line might well cost Rosecrans his position of command.

Option Three

Rosecrans could turn to an innovative solution and multiply the force of his mounted arm the latest weapon technology available.

Decision

Rosecrans decided to utilize a force multiplier: he would arm his cavalry with the most advanced weapons available and increase their rate of fire in battle. The weapon Rosecrans initially preferred was the five-shot Colt revolving rifle, but only three hundred of them were manufactured each month. He then decided to ask for ten thousand breech-loading carbines.

These weapons were more expensive for the army to purchase, and they required specialized ammunition that exacerbated supply problems. Some officers thought the carbines encouraged wasting ammunition since soldiers could fire faster. When Gen. Henry Halleck objected to the request, Rosecrans took his case to Secretary of War Edwin Stanton, who approved it.

Results/Impact

Beginning in mid-March Rosecrans began to receive the requested weapons. His cavalry command got 485 revolving rifles, 150 Sharps breech-loading carbines, 1,400 Gallagher carbines, 226 Smiths, and 500 Burnside carbines. The soldiers also received 6,000 of the newest pattern of Colt's revolving pistols. By the beginning of May all cavalry in the Army of the Cumberland had been rearmed with the most modern weapons available.[14]

The outcome of cavalry engagements changed dramatically following the increase in Union firepower. By April the Northern horsemen were holding their own in clashes with their Southern counterparts, and when the active phase of the Tullahoma Campaign began the Union cavalry would dominate the field.

After all Rosecrans's work toward rearming his cavalry, these troops ironically won their most complete victory at Shelbyville, where a saber charge swept a Confederate division from the town.

Alternative Scenario

What might have happened had Rosecrans continued to use the cavalry at his disposal even if the temporary result was constant harassment by Confederate cavalry? Waiting could have allowed him the opportunity to advance without additional mounted forces. We now know that, as the Vicksburg Campaign developed, Confederate cavalry was diverted from the Army of Tennessee to oppose Grant's forces. Eventually, this diminution of mounted opposition could have allowed Rosecrans to move forward in a campaign that depended on his superior infantry. In contrast, waiting for a possible lessening of opposition risked further irritating Secretary of War Edwin Stanton, who was anxious for the Army of the Cumberland to move.

The experience of Major General Grant in December 1862, when he abandoned his first thrust at Vicksburg after Brig. Gen. Earl Van Dorn's Confederate cavalry force destroyed his supply base at Holly Springs, Mississippi, shows the risks of operating without adequate cavalry to protect lines of supply. Grant minimized these pitfalls in his 1863 Vicksburg Campaign by advancing through Arkansas, where he knew there was no Confederate cavalry and where he could be supplied via the Mississippi River. With hindsight we know a similar opportunity would eventually be offered to Rosecrans.

Rosecrans Creates a Mounted Infantry Force

Situation

Rosecrans needed to secure his supply line, and he needed to gather information. Both of these objectives indicated he needed to strengthen his cavalry, and he was taking steps to carry out that critical decision by giving his mounted arm the best weapons available. The result of this choice could not be known in advance, and Rosecrans was a prudent commander. While moving to carry out one decision, he felt the need to provide a backup plan reinforcing the first decision.

Throughout much of the war, especially in the West, the Confederate cavalry had achieved many successes by fighting dismounted and on horseback. In part, the absence of traditional cavalry arms, especially carbines, dictated this style of fighting. The Confederate cavalry was noted for carrying double-barreled shotguns during the very early part of the war. While quite effective at close range, these weapons but did not allow the Rebel cavalry to compete in firepower with Union troopers carrying carbines. Imported Enfields and captured Springfield rifles were in greater supply than carbines, so Confederate cavalry, especially in the West, came to be armed with infantry rifles. Because a mounted man could not load these weapons, cavalrymen were trained to fight on foot when the enemy was to be engaged at long range.

This propensity for fighting on foot has led some historians to reach the false conclusion that Confederate cavalrymen in the West were really mounted infantrymen. Mounted infantry never fought on horseback, and they did not carry weapons such as revolvers that would allow them to fight while mounted. Members of the western Confederate cavalry were actually cross-trained and armed to function as either infantry or cavalry as the situation demanded.

As noted, Rosecrans badly needed to confront the Confederate cavalry since their effectiveness blocked his plans to advance farther.

Options

Rosecrans was already doing all he could to strengthen his cavalry. However, the problem was time. Rosecrans knew the war would not wait—either he moved or his opponent might. Rosecrans also knew the War Department would not wait indefinitely. Newspapers were already wondering why all the Union armies were motionless, and the War Department was sure to react to that expression of public opinion. Don Carlos Buell, Rosecrans's predecessor in command, had lost his position because he moved too slowly.

As a commanding officer, Rosecrans could follow a traditional path, trusting that his improved, newly armed cavalry would accomplish the tasks needed. On the other hand, he could try an innovative approach and create a new force of a different kind.

Option One

Rosecrans had some inkling that his rival Ulysses Grant was planning a campaign minimizing the role of cavalry. Grant could plan such a operation because his advance on Vicksburg could be supplied via the Mississippi River, which Confederate cavalry could not interdict. Thus Grant's infantry could advance down the west, or Arkansas, bank of the river, where Confederate cavalry was conspicuous by its absence. Rosecrans could try to develop a similar scheme, although the geography facing him did not offer a similar situation.

Option Two

Rosecrans could be innovative and call on established army procedures to create a mounted infantry force. This choice would solve the problem of time, since such a unit could be formed rapidly. The additional men and firepower would add force to the impetus Rosecrans's cavalry needed to impart to the campaign. In addition, this new force would not require the time necessary to train men and horses to operate as cavalry.

Decision

Rosecrans might have been influenced by the success of the Confederate model of cavalry trained to fight on foot as well as on horseback, but his response to his situation was to follow an old, established military tradition and create a unit of mounted infantry. These soldiers used horses to reach the battlefield, then dismounted and moved into battle to fight as infantry. Mounted

John Wilder.

infantry wore the blue uniform trim of the infantry and were organized into companies and regiments as infantry.

Rosecrans had to defend this choice to Gen. Henry Halleck, who shared the professional officer corps' prejudice against mounted infantry. For the general and others like him, mounted infantry made poor infantry and worse cavalry. Despite this bias, Rosecrans upheld his choice of options as the best available.

Results/Impact

One infantry brigade in the Army of the Cumberland was ripe for becoming a mounted unit. Col. John Wilder's brigade had spent the period from Christmas Day 1862, until New Year's Day 1863 chasing Gen. John Hunt Morgan. Morgan and his men were on the Christmas Raid, which destroyed miles of track on the Louisville & Nashville Railroad, including the lengthy trestles at Muldraughs Hill, Kentucky. Soldiers in this brigade had marched many miles over muddy roads, often sleeping in the rain, and had not once caught up with Morgan. Wilder and his men knew that two-legged creatures could not catch four-legged animals! On January 5, 1863, the brigade began another forty-mile march protecting a wagon train moving from Nashville to Murfreesboro. A month later in early February, when Rosecrans announced the idea of forming a brigade of mounted infantry, Wilder's men were pleased with their colonel's decision to volunteer his brigade.

Eli Lilly.

The regiments forming this brigade were the Seventeenth Indiana, the Seventy-Second Indiana, the Ninety-Eighth Illinois, and the 123rd Illinois. Eli Lilly's battery of light artillery, the Eighteenth Indiana Battery, was assigned to support the brigade. The men were led on a foraging expedition into Warren and DeKalb Counties in Tennessee, and they seized enough horses to mount the entire command. These horses were not fast enough or strong enough for use by cavalry, but they were good enough to provide transportation for Wilder's men.[15]

Although they were still infantry, Wilder's men had to learn something of life in the cavalry. It was necessary to learn the "army way" of caring for horses, using the necessary tack, and drilling to master the tasks of mounting, forming column, and marching in mounted ranks. Such training required the remainder of February and all of March, but Wilder's mounted infantry was ready to go into battle by April. In their first engagement with the enemy, at Snow Hill, Tennessee, on April 1, 1863, Wilder's men penetrated deep into territory held by their nemesis John Hunt Morgan. In this and all the rest of their engagements that spring, they were successful.

Forming a mounted infantry unit was a critical decision in that it was a deciding factor in turning the tide of battle in favor of the Union mounted forces, and in collecting the information Rosecrans needed to shape his decisive move beginning on June 23, 1863. When the active phase of the campaign began, Wilder's men played a key role in seizing Hoover's Gap and redi-

John McCown.

recting the focus of the entire campaign. Wilder's Brigade would continue shaping events through the Battle of Chickamauga and beyond.

Bragg Arrests Maj. Gen. John McCown

Situation

On December 30, 1862, as the Battle of Stones River opened, the Confederate left was to attack en echelon, rolling up the Union right. With each Confederate unit bearing to its right, the attack constantly gained numbers and momentum. Gen. John McCown commanded the division farthest to the left and was to open the action. The assault began approximately on time and was immediately successful, but McCown allowed his unit to drift to the left instead of leading it to its right. A gap then opened between McCown and the next unit in line. Early in the attack it became necessary for Bragg to commit reserves to plug the widening gap left by McCown's bungled advance.

In his battle report Bragg blamed McCown for starting late, although the assault had begun at about 6:20 a.m., still a half hour before actual sunrise. Rumors circulated that McCown had been drinking to excess, but this sort of hearsay was a staple of Civil War gossip whenever an explanation for failure was needed. No proof of the talk about McCown was brought forward at his court-martial.

McCown had previously commanded the Confederate defense of New Madrid, Missouri, and at Island No. 10. The loss of these positions had made him suspect in Bragg's eyes ever since the spring of 1862, yet when Bragg took command of what would become the Army of Tennessee, McCown was one of his division commanders.One of the most senior officers in terms of service, McCown had commanded the artillery corps of the state forces of Tennessee at the time of secession. He was also one of the first officers from those forces received into Confederate service. McCown's powerful political allies included Sens. Gustavus Henry and Landon Haynes of Tennessee.

McCown did not help his standing with Bragg by criticizing his commanding officer. In direct contravention of orders, McCown frequently dispatched his staff officers on missions outside the department to which he was assigned. In addition, he freely expressed his disgust with Bragg and other officers from the Cotton States.[16]

Options

McCown was neither an inefficient nor drunken. He was not an outstanding combat officer, but he was competent. Bragg could have found some duty commiserate with McCown's rank and moved him into a noncombat position. Another option was confronting McCown, who was Bragg's known critic, then crushing him and sending a message to all other officers who expressed dissatisfaction with their commander.

Option One

Bragg had led the Army of Tennessee long enough to evaluate his general officers' and most of his colonels' capacity for command. He had certainly been in Tennessee long enough to understand the politics of the state and the way political influence affected his army. Officers were available who were better prepared to lead a division in combat than McCown—A. P. Stewart being one of them. It is understandable that Bragg would want the best men in leadership positions. A consideration of the political forces at work outside the army, and a knowledge of how many of his other subordinates had ties to sources of political power, made McCown's quiet removal a workable solution to two problems. With this course of action, Bragg would replace an ineffective officer and silence a critic while maintaining peace with political figures and his own officer corps.

Option Two

Braxton Bragg's greatest strength as a commanding officer was his ability to instill discipline. He had performed excellently at Pensacola, Florida, in the opening phase of the war while overseeing the training of raw recruits assembling there. He had also proven his ability to organize an army when he was given command of the Confederate Army of Mississippi following Shiloh. By the time Bragg's command was called north to participate in the Battle of Shiloh, he had transformed inexperienced recruits into disciplined, effective soldiers. Bragg knew that discipline was crucial to the success of any military organization. The lack of restraint displayed by McCown and other critics who openly expressed negative opinions violated one of Bragg's basic values.

According to Bragg, maintaining discipline required making an example of those who refused to exercise self-control. An enlisted man should be assigned fatigue duty for a lack of discipline, while a major general should be arrested and dismissed. Order had to be maintained, no matter what public opinion might say.

Decision

With the Army of Tennessee settled into winter quarters except for its cavalry, Bragg ordered the arrest of General McCown and removed him from command. McCown's political supporters immediately urged him to demand a court-martial at which the charges against him could be contested. The trial took place on March 16, 1863, and the charges against McCown were upheld.

Results/Impact

The decision of the court-martial appeared to be a victory for Bragg; his authority and his ideas had been upheld, and a critic had been forced into obscurity. Yet appearances were quite deceiving. McCown's arrest initiated a sharp decline in confidence in Bragg and made obvious the growing split between the major general commanding and his subordinates.

No sooner had Bragg gotten his way in the McCown affair than he began a long and bitter quarrel with Gen. John Breckinridge. Breckinridge blamed Bragg for the large casualties his own men had suffered on the last day of the Battle of Stones River. The Orphan Brigade of Breckinridge's Division had advanced too far and encountered a maelstrom of artillery fire at McFadden's Ford. Breckinridge had subsequently criticized Bragg quite openly. Although Bragg's orders had called for the attack to seize the crest of a hill overlooking the ford, he had not intended for the troops to advance into the muzzles of the massed Union artillery defending the crossing. Bragg responded to this criticism by making negative remarks about Breckinridge's performance in his official report. Relations between the two men remained tense for the rest of the war.

Bragg also created friction in his relationship with Benjamin Franklin Cheatham, one of the most popular officers in the army. Cheatham was

John Breckinridge.

known to be intemperate, but he had promised to reform his conduct after being reprimanded by his corps commander, General Polk. Bragg ignored the action Polk had already taken and issued his own public censure of Cheatham.

Dissent became so pronounced that Jefferson Davis sent department commander Gen. Joseph Johnston to army headquarters at Tullahoma to evaluate the situation and take command of the army if necessary. Johnston's failure to replace Bragg only increased Bragg's feeling that he was overcoming his opponents and that his course of action was correct.[17]

The arrest of General McCown is a critical decision because it showed Bragg had no tolerance for critics and would crush them. Many subordinate officers reacted by deeming Bragg an overly harsh tyrant. McCown's apprehension brought into focus Bragg's inability to create a working relationship with officers who did not support him completely. The absence of a working leadership team made the Army of Tennessee dysfunctional and became a prime factor in the army's failure in the Tullahoma Campaign. The removal of General McCown may have been the most far-reaching decision Bragg made during the campaign since it irreparably damaged Bragg's ability to win his subordinate officers' cooperation.

Alternative Scenario

Option 1 deserves consideration as offering an alternative answer to the question of McCown's future. Forces underwent reorganization following the Battle of Stones River. During the Army of Tennessee's stay at Tullahoma, many men were discharged because of age and health, and many officers were reassigned to new duties. McCown could possibly have been transferred to a position in which he could serve without combat duty. This change would have created a vacancy in the command of McCown's Division. Bragg could then have promoted an officer of his choice while lessening the likelihood of a confrontation with officers who had powerful political allies.

Colonel Wilder Equips His Men with Technologically Advanced Rifles

Situation

Rosecrans had strengthened his cavalry by arming the troopers with breech-loading carbines and new Colt revolvers. He had increased the manpower of his mounted force by creating a brigade of mounted infantry that had proven itself effective in battle. Horses provided mobility that made Wilder's Brigade effective in penetrating enemy territory, scouting, gathering intelligence, and successfully reporting back to army headquarters. Wilder also wanted greater firepower. Using the standard issue Springfield rifle, soldiers could fire two to three rounds per minute. In strengthening the cavalry by technology (adopting the latest in weaponry), Rosecrans inspired Wilder to think along the same lines.

Wilder had a background and prewar career in technology. He had worked in a foundry in Columbus, Ohio, and, when the war began, he owned a company in Greensburg, Indiana, that built hydraulic machinery. Wilder had designed several of the machines his company produced, and he held patents for their designs. This involvement in technology reinforced his desire to make his unit the most effective possible and led him to ponder the best weapon with which to arm his command.[18]

Three repeating rifles had made their appearance by the winter of 1862–63: Colt produced a five-shot revolving rifle, Henry manufactured a sixteen-shot repeater, and Spencer had developed a seven-shot repeater.

Options

Option One

While Wilder wished to increase the efficiency of his command by securing advanced weapons, it was not mandatory that he take any such move. He could continue to arm his men with the standard infantry weapons; such a decision would be in keeping with accepted War Department practice. Securing ammunition and replacement weapons would not be a problem if the standard-issue weapons were kept. One of the regiments in Wilder's Brigade chose this option and asked for a transfer to a brigade armed in the traditional fashion.

Option Two

Wilder could seek out and adopt the most advanced and most suitable weapon available.

Decision

In consultation with the soldiers of his unit, Wilder adopted a repeating rifle that enhanced the brigade's firepower. Wilder's critical decision was to secure the most technologically advanced weapons for his command. However, a significant part of that decision was selecting the right weapon from those available.

The military model of the Colt revolving rifle was .54 caliber and used paper cartridges and percussion caps. Its slow reloading time slowed the rate of fire. Colt produced only three hundred of these weapons each month, and Rosecrans had already promised the entire production quota to the cavalry. Until the horsemen had all the Colt rifles they wanted, Wilder would have to wait his turn should this weapon be his choice.

The Henry repeater utilized a sixteen-round magazine located under the barrel. Metallic rounds were fed into the breech of the weapon when a lever forming part of the trigger guard was swung down and forward. Returning the trigger guard to its original position closed the breech and cocked the weapon. The weapon was .44 caliber and used a metallic cartridge. Its twenty-three moving parts, including some very small springs and screws, made it sensitive to dirt and difficult to field-strip. In 1863 the Henry was being produced in limited numbers.

The Spencer was a breech-loading rifle using a seven-round magazine inserted in the stock of the weapon. It used metallic rimfire cartridges in .52

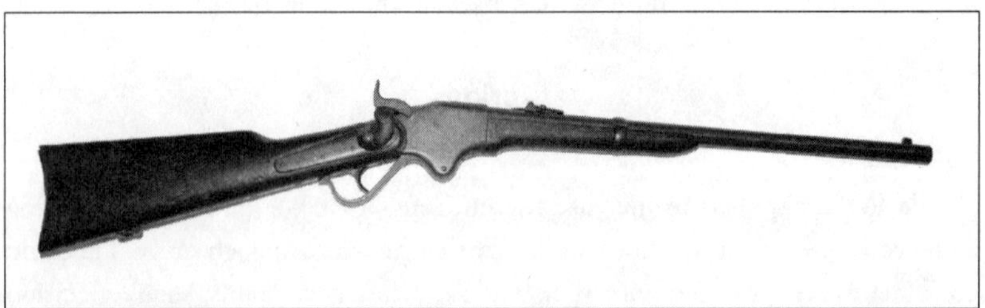

Spencer rifle.

caliber, and it had only seven moving parts, making it much easier to keep clean. In addition, the Spencer cost less than the Henry, and the Spencer company could fill orders rather quickly.[19]

Any of the available repeaters would give Wilder's Brigade superiority in firepower over a traditionally armed unit of equal, or even greater, size. What was the most suitable choice? The War Department would pay for the Colt revolving rifle, but the men of the command rejected that weapon for its use of paper cartridges. The Henry was too difficult to keep in order under field conditions. The Spencer, however, was easy to maintain, reliable to use, and available for prompt delivery from the manufacturer. The decision was made to adopt the Spencer.

Because the men were so enthusiastic about the Spencer, they agreed to sign promissory notes for the thirty-five-dollar purchase price. A set sum would be deducted from their pay each month. John Wilder's personal banker agreed to make available the sum needed for the purchase, and Wilder himself cosigned the note.[20] The Spencers arrived on May 15.

Result/Impact

Upon adopting repeating weapons, Wilder's Brigade immediately became the most powerful unit for its size in the western area of the war. In a scouting expedition at Liberty, Tennessee, and at Hoover's Gap, the brigade swept all opposition from the field, then held its position at Hoover's Gap against superior numbers. The Spencer-carrying men who went into action at Chickamauga achieved a similar result.

The long-term results of this decision were far-reaching. Infantry tactics began to change. To fire enough rounds to hold or to assault a position, it was no longer necessary to form infantry in a shoulder-to-shoulder line with men positioned two deep. Soldiers could be spread out in a looser formation, and the increased firepower would achieve the desired offensive or defensive result. At Hoover's Gap, Wilder took about 1,200 men into action and occupied a line about one thousand yards in length, much longer than would have been possible with Springfield muzzle-loading rifles. Soldiers armed with a Spencer could now fire and reload while lying on the ground, a feat nearly impossible with a muzzle-loading weapon. Wilder's men fought in a pouring rain at Hoover's Gap, but there are no recorded instances of a misfire since the Spencer used a metal cartridge. Repeating rifles using metal cartridges brought the development of a rapid-fire automatic weapon much closer to realization. Indeed, the adoption of the Spencer repeater forever changed the nature of warfare, and that process had its beginnings with John Wilder's critical decision.

Alternative Scenario

When Colonel Wilder assembled his soldiers to discuss the choice of rifle for rearming the brigade, the men were struck by the fact that the War Department would pay for the Colt revolving rifle. The cost of the alternative weapons, the Henry and the Spencer, would have to be born by the men themselves. Either of these firearms would cost more than two months' pay, and the soldiers had grave questions as to whether they could afford this investment. Many of the men had families who depended on their pay for their support.

What might have resulted from a decision to rearm with the Colt rifle? In the forays against the eastern flank of the Confederate line, all of which took place in dry weather, the Colts would likely have performed acceptably, increasing the rate of fire each soldier could deliver. The men of Wilder's Brigade might have been satisfied with their weapons as they rode into Hoover's Gap, but this time conditions were quite different—it was raining heavily.

It is a matter of record that the Lightning Brigade pushed the single squadron of the Confederate Second/Third Consolidated Kentucky out of the gap. But would the rate of reloading with paper cartridges have slowed in a heavy rain? Would misfires have occurred?

The *Official Records* say that on reaching the eastern end of the gap Wilder's Brigade took up defensive positions and made ready to confront the Confederate infantry approaching the field. In a pouring rain the Twentieth Tennessee made a charge on Lilly's Battery in the center of Wilder's line. Both Union and Confederate accounts agree that this attack came within twenty yards of the Union cannon.

If Wilder had chosen the Colt rifle, the defending soldiers would have had two fewer rounds with which to repel the attack (five rounds in the Colt, seven in the Spencer). Some of these rounds would likely have misfired because of the wet conditions. Would the Colt rifles then have run out of rounds just as the Confederates reached a distance from which they could make a final dash and overrun Lilly's guns?

Had the Confederate attack succeeded, Wilder conceivably would have needed to fall back on the following Union division. This action would have left the gap sealed by a Confederate brigade with another brigade coming up in support.

As a second alternative, John Wilder and the men of his brigade had a choice of four weapons when they were considering how to arm themselves as a unit of mounted infantry. The choice of the Spencer was not inevitable, and the choice of either of the other weapons presents an alternative scenario for the fighting at Hoover's Gap.

The established situation is that Wilder's Brigade advanced until encountering the Confederate vedettes. Then the lead regiment, the 123rd Illinois, broke into a gallop and pushed back the Southern force without giving its men time to get into formation. One squadron of the Second/Third Consolidated Kentucky Cavalry—about seventy-five men—opposed the 123rd Illinois. The men of the 123rd seized the "conical hill" overlooking the road to Fairfield, the location of the nearest Confederate camp, and were soon reinforced by Lilly's Battery and the other regiments of Wilder's Brigade. In the early afternoon the Confederate brigade led by William Bate arrived and attempted to retake the gap. The Twentieth Tennessee charged Lilly's Battery and came within twenty yards of the cannon before the fire of the 123rd Illinois drove it back.

What might have been the outcome of the fighting had Wilder's men not been armed with the Spencer repeaters? The brigade considered retaining the traditional infantry weapon, muzzle-loading Springfield rifles. One regiment of Wilder's original command made just that choice, and its soldiers were then "swapped" for a regiment from another brigade that wanted repeaters.

If Wilder had led a brigade armed with muzzle-loaders, the tactics these weapons forced on him would have prevented him from forming a battle line long enough to block and hold Hoover's Gap. Muzzle-loading weapons would have required Wilder to have a battle line composed of men standing shoulder to shoulder and two deep. Wilder led about 1,200 men into Hoover's Gap, and the battle line just described would have been 600 men in length and two deep. Such a line could have been outflanked by Bate's advance. Wilder's only alternative to a traditional battle line would have been to form an extended skirmish line. This, too, would have been vulnerable, and it might have suffered defeat. If this decision had been made, a different outcome at Hoover's Gap might have followed.

A consideration of these scenarios leads to the conclusion that Wilder's critical decision included not only arming his men with repeating weapons but also choosing the right weapon.

Rosecrans Uses His Mounted Infantry Against John Hunt Morgan's Position

Situation

Rosecrans needed his mounted forces to gather information, to bring in forage to alleviate his supply situation, to protect his line of communications, and to disrupt Bragg's plans by penetrating the area from which the Army of

Tennessee gathered its food. The opening weeks of 1863 brought only failure to the Union cavalry.

In January a Confederate cavalry force under Wheeler and Forrest attacked Dover, Tennessee, in an attempt to cut off the flow of supplies reaching Nashville via the Cumberland River. Though repulsed at Dover, the Confederate cavalry made numerous forays into the same area, seriously restricting the delivery of crucial goods to Rosecrans. In March Gen. Earl Van Dorn, seconded by Forrest, attacked a Union column of infantry, cavalry, and artillery at Thompson's Station. Col. John Coburn's Union force was decimated, losing over 1,600 of its 2,800 men. At the end of March Forrest attacked Brentwood, Tennessee, and captured the garrison there before moving on a stockade at the Harpeth River and repeating his success. In April the horsemen in gray flooded into Franklin for a raid. Forrest was then sent in pursuit of Col. Abel Streight, who was attempting to cut the railroad south of Chattanooga. In that storied pursuit Forrest succeeded in capturing all of Streight's force.

On the western end of the opposing lines the Union cavalry suffered defeat after defeat, reaching none of the objectives Rosecrans set. The Confederate cavalry under Van Dorn and Forrest were superior to the forces sent against them.

Options

Rosecrans would have to use some of his mounted force on both his flanks in order to screen his position and to gather intelligence about Confederate moves. There were options as to where the bulk of the horsemen would be used; west, against the Confederate's strongest cavalry or east, where conditions seemed to offer some Union advantages.

Option One

Rosecrans could continue to probe to the west because conditions had changed. In April, while Forrest was pursuing Streight, Van Dorn was shot by a jealous husband, Dr. Peters, at Spring Hill, Tennessee. Command of Confederate cavalry in the area devolved to Forrest. Forrest was then wounded in an attack by a disgruntled subordinate, Lieut. Willis Gould. With the two ranking officers out of the picture, Rosecrans had the option of using his mounted arm against proven soldiers who no longer had proven leaders in the top ranks.

Rosecrans could gain much by operating in the western area. His logistics network was more vulnerable there, and he had a good opportunity to gain intelligence about the deployment of Confederate infantry concentrated in that sector. Moreover, Rosecrans would have the opportunity of disrupting Bragg's supply network.

Option Two

Rosecrans could deploy his mounted arm to the eastern sector of the lines. The terrain was more rugged in that area and less suited for cavalry operations. Additionally, the Confederates did not draw any food from that sector. Furthermore, as the bulk of Confederate troops were placed more to the south and west, Union troops stationed in this area could gather less intelligence about the enemy's condition and plans. On the other hand, Rosecrans knew that John Hunt Morgan, the Confederate commander in the eastern sector of the lines, lacked Van Dorn's and Forrest's reputation for instilling disciplinc. Thus thc Confcdcratc cavalry in that location might be less well prepared. Also, thhough Rosecrans's men had less opportunity to gather intelligence about Confederates' strength and movement if they were stationed in this area, they would still have a great opportunity to scout roads toward Chattanooga that outflanked the Army of Tennessee's position.

Decision

Rosecrans exerted additional force against the eastern Confederate flank, especially the positions held by the command of John Hunt Morgan. The equipment of Morgan's men was thought to be inferior to that of the units commanded by Van Dorn. In addition, the morale of Morgan's men had sunk during the winter; their commander spent most of his time with his new bride and very little with his troops in the field.

Result/Impact

From their first attempt, the men commanded by Rosecrans began to have success in the eastern area. On March 18 a force comprised largely of infantry had moved as far east as Gainesville, Tennessee, on a scout. Approached by elements of Morgan's command, the Union force withdrew to a defensive position at Milton. Unsurprisingly, Morgan's cavalry could not displace infantry from a defensive position, but Morgan withdrew because his men ran out of ammunition. His inattention to detail in this instance encouraged Rosecrans to send his mounted arm against the east wing of the Confederate position.

On April 1 Wilder's newly formed mounted infantry moved against Liberty and Snow Hill, Tennessee. The horsemen were confronted by Confederates commanded by Gen. John Wharton, but Wilder moved boldly against them. Wharton took a defensive stance, so Wilder was free to collect five hundred horses and mules, eighty-six tons of hay and forage, four thousand bushels of corn, and a large contingent of African Americans who accompanied the expedition back to Murfreesboro, where they had been promised paid employment.

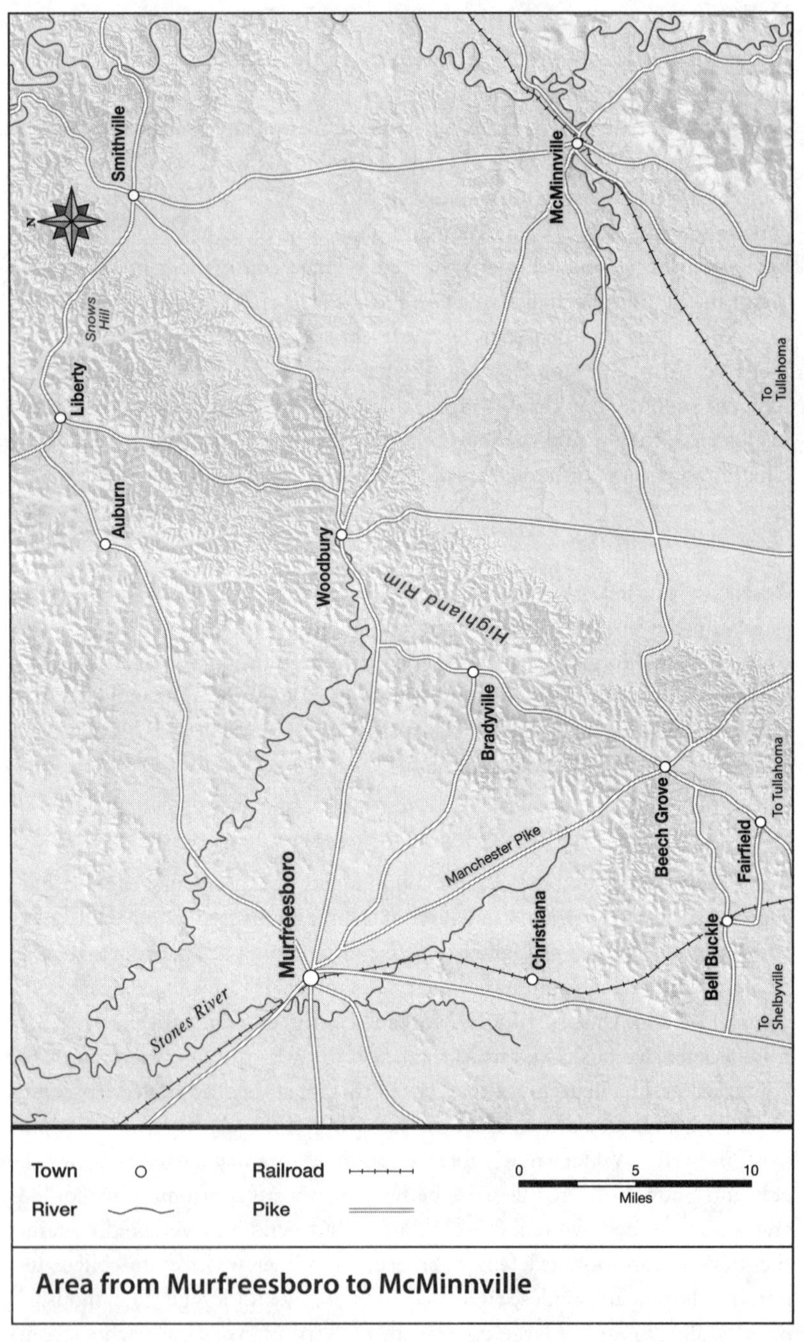

Area from Murfreesboro to McMinnville

Following up on this success, Wilder and 1,700 cavalry under Colonel Minty moved against Morgan's headquarters at McMinnville. Although supported by infantry, the mounted force moved far in advance of their support and fought on their own. The horsemen penetrated to within two miles of McMinnville before they encountered any pickets. Brushing these aside, they charged into town and began a search for Morgan himself. Morgan narrowly escaped, but his headquarters establishment was captured, a large amount of camp equipment was burned, Confederate units were scattered, and Mrs. Morgan herself briefly came into Union custody.

Throughout the month of May, Union mounted units penetrated Morgan's area of command at will. While they did not damage Confederate logistics, they did gather information about the road network that would be of major importance to Rosecrans in deciding which direction to advance. The use of Rosecrans's mounted arm in the eastern sector revealed several good roads available to him by which he could pass beyond Bragg's right flank and place the Army of the Cumberland between the Army of Tennessee and Chattanooga.

Alternative Scenario

Confederate cavalry around Spring Hill were closer to Murfreesboro and were the greatest threat to foraging parties and to supply boats operating on the Cumberland River. Thus Rosecrans could have continued to concentrate on the western area while using just enough force against Wheeler and Morgan to keep them in check. Such a decision would have deprived Rosecrans of information that was crucial in helping him make the critical decision to move against Bragg's right flank. However, this choice would have convinced Bragg to continue neglecting the conditions on his right flank because his left seemed threatened.

Jefferson Davis and Bragg Disperse Men from the Army of Tennessee

Situation

As the spring of 1863 passed it became clear to the Confederate War Department in Richmond that General Bragg had adopted a purely defensive strategy for the Army of Tennessee. Developments in other smilitary departments revealed a pressing need for soldiers to be sent elsewhere if they could be spared. The most critical need was in Mississippi, where Vicksburg was under attack by Maj. Gen. Ulysses Grant. By May 16 the Confederate defeat

Jefferson Davis.

at Champion's Hill made a siege of Vicksburg inevitable. The only hope for the garrison of the town was for Gen. Joseph Johnston to raise a sufficient force in the rear of Grant's lines to so threaten him that the siege would be lifted in order to face the new threat. With great good luck, Johnston might also coordinate a move between the Vicksburg garrison and the relief force that would catch Grant between the two forces.

Political pressure to alleviate the situation in Mississippi, as well as the obvious military conditions, increased. Influential voices in the Confederate Congress called for a spirited defense of the state and found a sympathetic listener in President Davis, whose home was in Mississippi. Indeed, his plantation was located near Vicksburg. Responding to both the military and political situations, Jefferson Davis asked Bragg to send troops to Mississippi. Bragg quickly responded by offering the infantry division commanded by John Breckinridge, supplemented by two thousand cavalry led by Gen. William Hicks "Red" Jackson. The cavalry was badly needed in Mississippi; there were only two regiments of regular cavalry in the state, supplemented by a few home guard and state troop units.

Breckinridge had constantly criticized Bragg since the Battle of Stones River. Dispatching his command to Mississippi would get rid of an antagonist and reinforce Johnston. Bragg was also well aware that earlier in the spring Davis had received several suggestions that Bragg be replaced as commander of the Army of Tennessee. Davis had remained loyal to Bragg, and now the favor was being repaid.

Options

With limited manpower the Confederates had not been able to hold all of their territory that came under attack. From the first of the war, however, attempting to do so had been an unofficial policy leading to disastrous military results. In May 1863 the unfortunate results of that practice were clear, and the Davis administration could have considered a change. At any rate, three options were available to the Confederate leadership.

Option One

The Confederates could attempt to hold Mississippi by concentrating enough manpower there to make Grant abandon his siege of Vicksburg. In round numbers, Grant had sixty thousand men under his immediate command. He was being supplied by river and by foraging in his rear. Even when Breckinridge's division was sent from Tennessee, Joseph Johnston's total force numbered only about twenty thousand. Some additional reinforcements did arrive from other locations, but none of them brought their artillery. Instead, the big guns traveled a circuitous route by rail.

An attempt to save Vicksburg would require that the entire Army of Tennessee be sent to Mississippi, placing some fifty thousand Confederate troops in Grant's rear and the garrison of Vicksburg in his front. This concentration of manpower would have a reasonable chance of forcing Grant to abandon the siege of Vicksburg and engage in a campaign of maneuver that might last for several weeks. However, this concentration would leave Middle Tennessee vulnerable and the door to Chattanooga wide open.

An alternate plan of concentration would have been to take most of the cavalry from the Army of Tennessee, between fourteen thousand and sixteen thousand horsemen, and send the bulk of them to operate against Grant's rear and to set up rolling blockades on the Mississippi River. William Hicks Jackson and Nathan Bedford Forrest, as well as many lower-ranking officers, were thoroughly familiar with the area and could effectively bring pressure to bear in the rear of the Union army.

Option Two

Confederates could attempt to hold Middle Tennessee by concentrating all forces in the western area to oppose Rosecrans. This course of action would mean abandoning Mississippi without a fight, and this would have met strong political opposition. However, Bragg was a more aggressive commander than Joseph Johnston. With urging from Richmond, he might make a successful defense of his area.

This option required comparative analysis of the military importance of Mississippi and Middle Tennessee. The loss of Vicksburg would allow midwestern farmers unfettered access to the port of New Orleans and the markets of the East Coast and Europe. A political and military advantage for the Union would then have resulted, quietening midwesterners' grumbling about the effect of the war on the local economy. Vicksburg, however, did not offer a pathway deeper into the heart of the Confederacy and was not of exceptional value as a military post.

Present-day historians usually argue that Vicksburg provided a vital supply point allowing food to flow from Texas and Louisiana into the eastern part of the Confederacy. Yet this is a somewhat overblown concept. Vicksburg had no rail connections with the West and only limited water connections. Equally, no major rail link gave Vicksburg access to the rest of the Confederate states east of the Mississippi River. The Confederacy survived the loss of the city very well for almost two more years of war, although both political leaders and civilians talked constantly about the "fall of Vicksburg."

The loss of Middle Tennessee cost the Confederacy manufacturing capacity, food production, and supplies of horses, mules, and potential recruits. The loss of such a large swath of territory was more hurtful to morale in the South than was the loss of Vicksburg. Following this line of reasoning, the second option would concentrate forces in Middle Tennessee to take the offensive against Rosecrans or, at least, to mount a firmer defense. Joseph Johnston and the men he had collected at Jackson, Mississippi, would be brought to Tennessee, and Bragg's lines would be lengthened and strengthened. Such a concentration would greatly narrow the manpower gap Bragg faced in Tennessee. It might also result in a prolonged campaign, one that might not reach the gates of Chattanooga.

Option Three

The Rebels could attempt to hold Mississippi and Middle Tennessee by shifting manpower to meet emergencies in either or both areas.

Decision

Confederate forces attempted to hold both Mississippi and Middle Tennessee by shifting manpower from Tennessee to Mississippi. This decision was in keeping with the Confederacy's long-standing practice of holding all of its territory against multiple invading forces.

Result/Impact

The force collected by Joseph Johnston accomplished nothing, never reaching the size that would have made it effective. Bragg found his line easily outflanked on his right and was forced to retreat. The division led by Breckinridge arrived too late to assist in Mississippi and did not return to Tennessee until the Tullahoma Campaign was over. Both Vicksburg and Middle Tennessee were lost, and the occupation of Chattanooga opened the way to Atlanta in 1864.

Alternative Scenario

An alternative scenario must posit a change in the Confederacy's basic war policy, and it is therefore difficult to conceive of one without descending into "alternative history." But it is not unreasonable to consider that giving up territory in Mississippi and concentrating forces in Tennessee might have created an opportunity for stopping Rosecrans while permitting a Union victory in Mississippi. Following a Union success in Mississippi and a Confederate victory in Tennessee, an opportunity might arise for a Confederate advance into northern Mississippi or against Memphis. Either one would have again blocked the Mississippi River to midwestern commerce.

No Replacement Is Named When Forrest Is Disabled

Situation

On April 28 Col. Abel Streight began a raid designed to take him far behind Confederate lines to destroy part of the Western & Atlantic Railroad linking the Army of Tennessee with Atlanta. This move would not disturb the delivery of food to Bragg's men, as no food came up that line. Yet it would sever the link that delivered ordnance supplies. The target of Streight's expedition was Rome, Georgia, where the W&A crossed the Chattahoochee River.

Nathan Bedford Forrest and his command were skirmishing with Brig. Gen. Grenville Dodge's Union force near Florence, Alabama, when a scout brought Forrest news that a column of cavalry screened by Dodge's men had broken away to the south and east and were heading for the rear of Bragg's troops. Forrest immediately moved in pursuit with part of his force. During the next six days Forrest constantly battered the rear guard of the raiders, compelled the group to stop and deploy, and used every trick and strategy his fertile mind could devise to keep Streight's sleep-deprived men on the move while part of his own unit rested. On May 3, Forrest, with 600 men, convinced Streight, who had 1,700, to surrender.

Forrest returned to Spring Hill, Tennessee, the hero of the hour for the South. He also found himself in command of the cavalry on Bragg's left. Gen. Earl Van Dorn had gone once too often into the most dangerous territory any soldier can enter, the bedroom of another man's wife, and had been shot by a jealous husband.

Forrest reviewed the events leading to Streight's surrender and identified some personnel changes he thought would improve the efficiency of his command. One of these changes involved reassigning Lieut. Willis Gould to another post. During the pursuit of Streight a skirmish had been fought at Days Gap, Alabama, during which Gould commanded a section of artillery. Streight's attack had overrun Gould's unit and captured its guns. The guns were recovered two days later, but Forrest held the loss against Gould. The commander felt the lieutenant had mishandled his guns again during a June 4 reconnaissance toward Franklin, Tennessee. Gould came to see Forrest to protest his transfer, considering it a slight on his ability and integrity.[21]

In the ensuing interview Gould shot Forrest with a small-caliber pocket pistol and Forrest stabbed Gould with a pocketknife. Dr. J. H. Wilkes examined Forrest's wound and diagnosed it as fatal; the shot had probably penetrated a kidney. This diagnosis changed when Dr. J. B. Cowan, Forrest's personal physician, arrived on the scene. Cowan found that the small pistol ball had struck the hip bone but had not damaged it, sp the danger for Forrest was infection of the wound during the hot weather. To minimize this risk Forrest was ordered to rest in bed for several days and then to stay out of the saddle for several more.

While Forrest was fit enough to deal with paper work and routing headquarters matters, he was in no condition to lead cavalry in the field. Forrest was accustomed to lead from the front, and his men were accustomed to him doing so. That leadership would be absent during a critical period of the Tullahoma Campaign.

While brigade and regimental commanders under Forrest were competent, none of them possessed the charisma needed to keep their men functioning at the highest level for an extended period of time. Bragg and Wheeler considered who might assume Forrest's role and found no one. Since Forrest was still able to perform routine duties at headquarters, no replacement was named to exercise active field command.

Options

Today the obvious, and only, option would be to issue the order transferring the junior officer. This event, however, occurred in a very different time. The Confederate army reflected the values of the society from which it was drawn, and one of those values insisted that every man be ready and willing to defend his actions to another when called on to do so. Forrest and Gould were following well-established social norms even though those norms were not appropriate for military decisions.

Option One

Wheeler could temporarily take command of the cavalry on the western flank of the Army of Tennessee. Although it might not promote a higher level of activity on the part of the horsemen, this consolidation of command would lead to better coordination of forces in the opening days of the Tullahoma Campaign.

Option Two

While Forrest could retain overall command of his wing of cavalry, an acting field commander could be named as well. For example, Brig. Gen. Frank Armstrong in Spring Hill, Tennessee, was an experienced and active officer who had made a good record for himself in the war. Armstrong had experience in conducting raids behind enemy lines, and he was a professional soldier well schooled in the matters of scouting and screening an army.

Option Three

Bragg could decide to do nothing since Forrest was technically fit to retain command.

Frank Armstrong.

Decision

Bragg took no action to replace Forrest. The commander of the western wing of the cavalry was not able to return to field duty until June 24.

Result/Impact

Forrest's wounding removed the most aggressive and daring of the Confederate cavalry commanders from command just as Rosecrans was ready to make his forward move. From the time Forrest was shot until the beginning of the Tullahoma Campaign, the activity of the Confederate cavalry in the western sector slacked almost to a standstill. When the Union cavalry made its move, the Confederate response was disjointed. The forces in Forrest's command did little to hinder the enemy's advance and allowed Bragg's attention to be drawn to the west when the real threat was to the east. This inactivity allowed the free advance of the Union cavalry force and deprived Bragg of intelligence that could have allowed him to more accurately assess the situation.

This disjointed state of operations would continue until June 28, with Wheeler fighting a disastrous engagement at Shelbyville. Wheeler accepted battle in part because it was thought that Forrest needed to cross the Duck River at that place in order to rejoin the Confederate concentration at Tullahoma.

The quarrel between Gould and Forrest was a personal decision with important strategic consequences. Thus it may justifiably be discussed as influencing a critical decision of the Tullahoma Campaign.

Alternative Scenario

Forrest would not have suffered a disabling wound if he had refused to discuss a transfer with Lieutenant Gould. This supposition provides a possible fourth course of action leading to an alternative scenario.

It is reasonable to assume that Forrest, as an active field commander, would likely have spotted and firmly opposed Stanley's advance from Christiana toward Eagleville, Tennessee. Such opposition would have quickly revealed the move for what it was—a feint. Bragg would thus have had a clear indication that the main Union blow was directed toward his right. With this information he would have confronted additional options, including the possibility of offensive action.

Steven Woodworth contends that Bragg intended Polk to make an attack from Shelbyville north. Such an assault would have threatened McCook at Liberty Gap and offered a chance to move against Murfreesboro. An aide-de-camp to Bragg recorded that such a proposal was withdrawn less than a hour after its proffer on June 26 because Bragg lacked reliable intelligence when he made the proposal. Had Forrest been able to provide accurate information two or three days earlier, the strategic situation would possibly have been quite different.[22]

Bragg Strips His Right Flank of Cavalry

Situation

Ever since Morgan had occupied his section of the Confederate cavalry line, he had kept a chain of pickets and scouts beyond the right of his main line and extending into Kentucky. These troops brought some useful intelligence to Morgan at his headquarters at McMinnville, Tennessee. They also kept up contact with the guerrilla forces harassing the Louisville & Nashville Railroad, and they allowed Morgan to send small parties of his men back into their home territory to remount themselves and occasionally bring out recruits. The reports these soldiers brought to Morgan encouraged him to think another raid into the Bluegrass region would further damage the L&N and allow the gathering of men and supplies. This chain of scouts also fed the dissatisfaction felt by many of Morgan's troops concerning their situation in Tennessee. More and more men urged their officers to lead them "home to Kentucky," and by May 1863 one of Morgan's brigades had its headquarters at Albany, Kentucky.[23]

Morgan had enjoyed a winter of personal satisfaction in the company of his new bride, Mattie Ready, whom he had married just before Christmas 1862. The newlyweds were having such a good time of it that even the citizens of McMinnville became disgusted with the obvious lack of attention paid to military matters, especially to the condition of the men in the field. For example, the regiment stationed at Woodbury, on the main road from McMinnville to Murfreesboro, ran out of oats and fodder, leaving the horses to exist on only three ears of corn a day. Soon the horses became too weak to allow the troopers to do scouting duty.[24]

On February 13 Morgan's headquarters staff gave a dance in honor of General and Mrs. Morgan. By this time so many in McMinnville were upset with the lack of discipline among Morgan's men—soldiers had burned fence rails and raided chicken houses and pigpens—that the local ladies refused to attend the party. The men in attendance outnumbered the women by eight to one.

Morgan had also endured a winter of military embarrassment. Union mounted forces, including Wilder's mounted infantry armed with the new Spencer rifles, had battered his command repeatedly. Morgan had fled only a short distance ahead of Union cavalry overrunning his headquarters.

Moreover, he had felt the ignominy of having his bride briefly held as a prisoner. The psychological factor of seeking to regain his status and reputation must be considered along with the effect military intelligence had on Morgan's decision to propose a raid into Kentucky.[25]

Morgan's official reason for his proposed raid was as follows: to prevent Union troops currently guarding the L&N Railroad from reinforcing Rosecrans, to make a feint at the lightly guarded supply base of Louisville, and to distract the commander of Union troops in eastern Kentucky from moving against East Tennessee. Morgan presented his plan to General Wheeler, who then took the request to Bragg.

Bragg recognized that the weather had made all the roads leading from Murfreesboro to his positions passable, and that the military situation in Mississippi meant Washington officials were pressuring Rosecrans to make an offensive move. By this time sickness, defeats in battle, and detachments to Mississippi had reduced Bragg's cavalry force from about 16,000 to 9,000. For these reasons Bragg was reluctant to authorize the raid, but he finally agreed to allow Morgan to take 1,500 men on the expedition. Morgan replied by asking to be allowed to take 2,000, and this increase was agreed to. Upon receiving permission to move, he took his entire command of 2,500 with him, leaving the Confederate right very weak in cavalry. Indeed, the only troopers left behind were those Morgan thought unable to make the raid. These included men who were sick and those whose horses were unfit for service. The only organized force Morgan left behind was the First/Third Consolidated Kentucky commanded by Col. John R. Butler.[26]

Wheeler also moved cavalry from the right. Perhaps because he thought a spoiling attack would delay Rosecrans, or perhaps in connection with the move being made by Morgan, Wheeler concentrated the bulk of his remaining force at Shelbyville in preparation for a raid toward Nashville and the vital Louisville & Nashville rail link.[27] One regiment, the First/Third Consolidated Kentucky, was left to cover the approaches to both Hoover's Gap and Liberty Gap. The reasons for Wheeler's move are unclear since he filed no report about the matter. However, the quote from Dodson in footnote 14 is based on material Wheeler provided Dodson following the war.

Options

Clearly, Bragg had three possible responses to Morgan's request to raid into Kentucky. Bragg could refuse and keep his cavalry in place, he could agree and weaken his mounted force on his right, or he could allow a limited operation with Morgan taking part of his cavalry north.

Option One

Bragg could have refused to authorize Morgan's raid and Wheeler's move to Shelbyville. With the improved road conditions as summer came to Middle Tennessee, it should have been no surprise that Rosecrans would begin a campaign. Bragg had committed himself to a passive defense of the line of the Duck River, but even a passive defense requires a cavalry screen. Bragg also knew the ability of the Union mounted forces was increasing as these men were rearmed and reorganized. Thus he had the option to opt for a safe, prudent choice and keep his cavalry intact on his right flank.

Option Two

Bragg could allow his eastern flank to be stripped of cavalry. Given the activity of Union cavalry in the area during the past several weeks, this move would be very risky, but the choice was available if Bragg wished to take it.

Option Three

Morgan could be allowed use part of his 2,500 available men to make a limited raid on the Louisville & Nashville Railroad. This option would allow Bragg to continue to screen his right flank, and it would provide Wheeler cover for a raid south of the Cumberland River toward the eastern outskirts of Nashville. Such a move by Wheeler would cover the main roads leading east from Murfreesboro and place Confederate cavalry in the vicinity of the Union infantry camps, where intelligence could be gathered concerning the enemy's future moves.

Decision

Bragg authorized Morgan to make the proposed raid with a smaller force, but Morgan disobeyed orders, taking his entire command of 2,500 men. This left Wheeler with 930 troopers to defend the right flank of Bragg's position, and these, for reasons not made entirely clear in the records, were moved to the center of the line. In the absence of a documentary record, it is impossible to evaluate the reasons why Bragg chose this option.[28]

Result/Impact

The most obvious result, and the one most historians focus on, was Morgan's disastrous raid into Indiana and Ohio as he disobeyed his orders and moved far beyond the limits permitted for his operation. The destruction of Morgan's command drew, and still draws, a great deal of attention and comment.

However, the loss of 2,500 cavalrymen was not a disastrous blow to the Confederate cause. The picturesque nature of Morgan's venture, and his presence for a few days in an area that had never before hosted active military operations, provides a good story for writers to recount. Even so, this result was not critical for the progress of the war. The truly important result of Bragg's decision to strip his eastern flank of cavalry was that Rosecrans was able to advance unopposed and without Bragg knowing of his progress until Thomas's Corps was behind the right flank of the infantry line of the Army of Tennessee.

During the advance of the Army of the Cumberland Crittenden's Corps encountered only two Confederate cavalrymen, both of them captured while sleeping on the porch of a store. Thomas encountered one squadron of the First/Third Consolidated Kentucky (CSA) during his advance through Hoover's Gap, and McCook brushed aside the second squadron of the same regiment during his advance on Liberty Gap. The only response to the Union advance was in the area north and west of Shelbyville. There, General Stanley led the Union cavalry in a feint that successfully drew Bragg's attention while Rosecrans made his major thrust to the east toward Manchester.[29]

By stripping his right flank of cavalry, Bragg denied himself all intelligence of Rosecrans's move and deprived himself of the ability to slow the Union advance until he could concentrate his infantry to oppose it effectively. Leaving the eastern flank bare of cavalry and allowing Rosecrans to penetrate beyond Bragg's flank was a critical decision indeed.

Alternative Scenario

Given the condition of Morgan's command, it is questionable just how effective these men would have been in spotting and slowing Rosecrans's advance when it began on June 24. But if Bragg had refused to allow Morgan to make the raid, and if Bragg had concentrated his cavalry to more effectively cover his right—both reasonable moves—a different outcome to the Tullahoma Campaign is conceivable.

Closer observation of the Army of the Cumberland would have allowed Bragg to gather intelligence indicating Rosecrans intended to move east. With this warning Bragg would then have had motive to shift infantry to block Hoover's Gap so that a significant engagement resulted. The time lost to Rosecrans during such an engagement could have allowed Polk to concentrate against McCook at Liberty Gap and force him back, thus threatening to cut off Thomas. As a cautious commander, Thomas would then have faced the prospect of falling back toward Murfreesboro to protect his position. The campaign might have ended with Rosecrans still in the vicinity of Murfreesboro.

Given the state of mind concerning Thomas at the War Department, failure to take the offensive could have led to Rosecrans being relieved of command. How this would have affected developments for the rest of 1863 is a matter of conjecture.

CHAPTER 2

DURING THE CAMPAIGN

Before dawn broke on June 23 Rosecrans set his cavalry in motion, moving south and west to draw the Confederates' attention to that area. The Army of the Cumberland had been halted 169 days, but now action was to be swift. The infantry moved out in the early morning darkness of June 24. During the night of June 23–24 rain began to fall. Near-constant rainfall for the next ten days turned roads into quagmires, flooded streams, and bogged down wagons and artillery. The rain would play an important role in the development of the campaign.

Wilder Disregards Orders and Holds the Mouth of Hoover's Gap

Situation

Wilder had received orders the night of June 23 to move out the Manchester Pike in the direction of Hoover's Gap at dawn on June 24. The mounted infantry brigade was to act as the advance guard and screen for the advance of Thomas's Corps. Wilder had his command on the road by 4:00 a.m., only to find the men riding through rain that slowly increased in intensity. With few breaks, this precipitation was to last for the entire ten days of the Tullahoma Campaign. Wilder was camped on the southeast side of Murfreesboro and was to advance six miles before the first of the Fourteenth Corps infantry,

George Thomas.

Maj. Gen. Joseph J. Reynolds's division, took the road. At staggered intervals Maj. Gen. Lovell H. Rousseau's and Maj. Gen. James Negley's divisions followed. By 10:00 a.m. Wilder had reached the northern mouth of Hoover's Gap, eleven miles from Murfreesboro.[1]

Hoover's Gap is more like a ramp than a gap. Over a distance of four miles the floor of the gap rises approximately eight hundred feet in elevation, while the hills on either side of the gap are two to three hundred feet higher than the floor. At the community of Beech Grove the road debouches from Hoover's Gap to cross the valley of the Garrison Fork of the Duck River. It then proceeds across intervening ridges for almost four miles before ascending the rest of the way to the top of the Highland Rim via Matt's Hollow. From Beech Grove a road runs south to the community of Fairfield, where a Confederate infantry division commanded by Maj. Gen. Alexander Peter Stewart was encamped.

At the point where the road to Fairfield separated from the Manchester Pike was a steep hill on which the community cemetery was located. Farther back toward Murfreesboro three roads that could be used by infantry passed over the hills in the direction of Fairfield and Wartrace.[2]

Wilder reached the Murfreesboro end of Hoover's Gap unopposed and unobserved. For that day, Confederates had abandoned their normal observation post between the gap and Murfreesboro because the rain limited visibility to near zero. As the mounted infantry rode into the gap, they encountered one squadron of the Confederate First/Third Consolidated Ken-

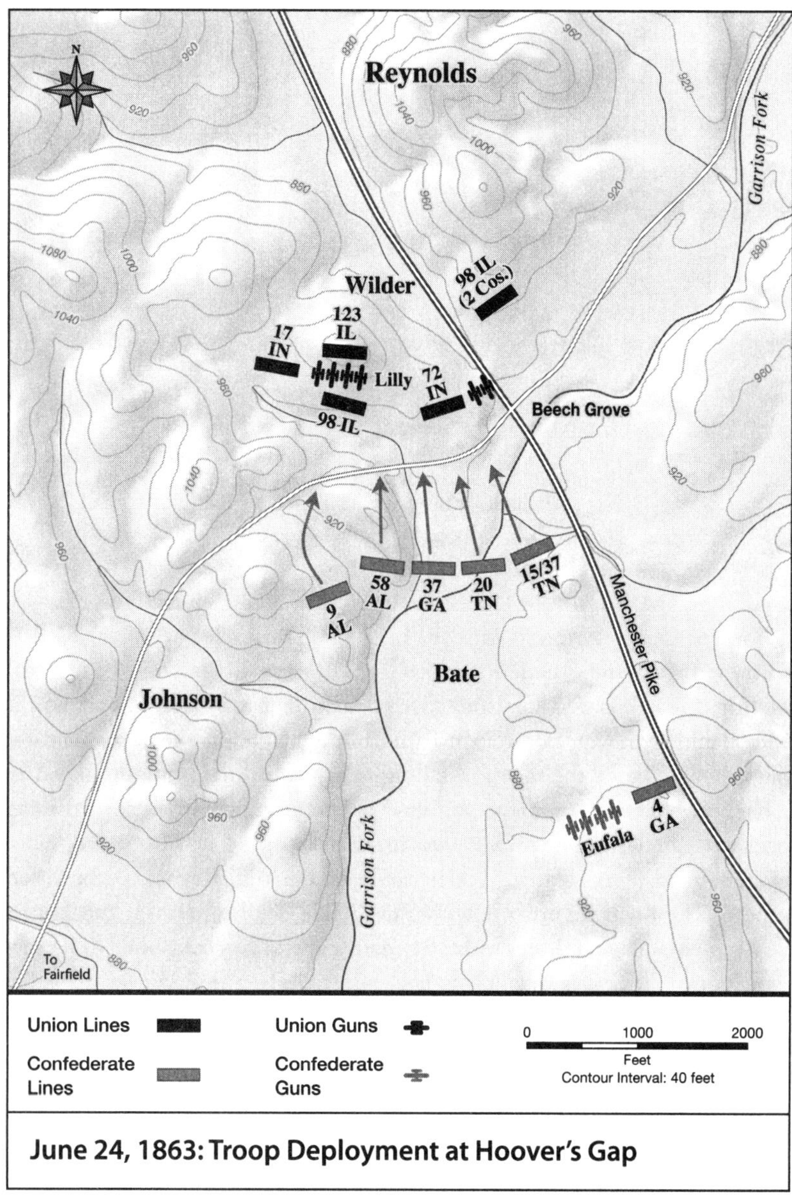

June 24, 1863: Troop Deployment at Hoover's Gap

tucky Cavalry, which Wilder's men had given rough treatment three weeks earlier in a skirmish near Liberty, Tennessee. Surprised, badly outnumbered, and outgunned, the Southern horsemen were quickly overrun. Most of their number were captured, but nine men escaped to tell the Rebels in Fairfield, "The Yankees are coming."[3]

Alexander P. Stewart.

Major General Stewart sent the brigade of Brig. Gen. William B. Bate to try to rectify the situation at Hoover's Gap while his second brigade, that of Brig. Gen. Bushrod Johnson, covered the other roads leading across the hills flanking the gap. Bate soon found himself fighting an enemy that was partially hidden by the sheets of falling rain yet still managing to unload an amazing volume of gunfire. The sound of the fighting carried several miles back to Reynolds, whose infantry was making slow progress through the mud-clogged road. Fearing that Wilder would be overrun, Reynolds sent a staff officer to him with an order to withdraw. Wilder felt he knew the capabilities of his men and their weapons better than General Reynolds did, so he sent word back that he was well able to hold his ground. In this, Wilder proved to be right. When General Thomas reached Wilder a few hours later, Thomas shook Wilder's hand and said, "You have saved the lives of a thousand men by your gallant conduct today. I didn't expect to get this gap for three days."[4]

Options

Option One

Wilder could obey the order. His immediate superior officer was Joseph Jones Reynolds, a major general and West Point graduate who had Rosecrans's confidence. In contrast, John Wilder was a colonel with no formal military training. If Wilder fell back and the Confederates sealed the mouth of Hoover's Gap, causing a delay in the Union advance and, perhaps, a signifi-

J. J. Reynolds.

cant engagement, the responsibility would have fallen on Reynolds. If Wilder disobeyed the order and his command was defeated, the responsibility would be his alone, potentially ending his military career.

Option Two

Wilder could disobey the order. Wilder knew the fighting capacity of his men and he knew the firepower produced by the Spencer rifles. This knowledge, which Reynolds lacked, gave Wilder the confidence to ignore the order and to hold his ground. Wilder's experience with the new technology of the repeating rifle gave him the basis for making a decision that differed from the conclusion Reynolds reached with his traditional training and experience.

Impact/Results

The important results of disobeying Reynolds's orders were as Thomas stated: time and lives had been saved.

In a larger sense, Wilder's decision changed the nature of warfare. The traditional line of battle would begin to give way to the deployment tactics of today: strongpoints linked by fields of fire. Fewer men were needed to hold a position since technology had provided a "force multiplier." During the engagement at Hoover's Gap, the course of war began to move away from the traditions stretching back to the introduction of firearms, and the tactics of modern war were born.

Rosecrans Alters His Plan to Adapt to the Changed Circumstances

Situation

As originally planned, Rosecrans intended to send his cavalry to the south and west to draw Bragg's attention to the Confederate left flank. Reinforcing this feint, McCook's Twentieth Corps was to march south from Murfreesboro to Christiana and then turn east and south to reach Liberty Gap. From that position McCook could threaten a route leading from Liberty Gap to Bell Buckle and on to Shelbyville, or McCook could move via Bell Buckle to Wartrace and on to Tullahoma. The movement of the cavalry and McCook was a diversion to distract Bragg.

Maj. Gen. Thomas L. Crittenden's Twenty-First Corps was to be the focus of the campaign. His unit was to move east from Murfreesboro and then turn southeast to reach Manchester. Thomas was to support Crittenden by an advance through Hoover's Gap. When Crittenden reached Manchester he was to move east to cross Elk River and then move south to sever the Nashville & Chattanooga Railroad, cutting the Confederate supply line and forcing Bragg to fight when and where Rosecrans chose.

The cavalry and McCook had carried out their part of the plan as ordered. Crittenden had not been able to do so, through no fault of his own. Shortly after midnight on June 24, just as the Union infantrymen were breaking camp to take their assigned roads, rain began to fall. Heavy rain continued with few

Alexander McDowell McCook.

intervals for the next ten days, so that The Tullahoma Campaign would be fought in conditions seldom seen in Middle Tennessee at that season of the year. The road Crittenden was to follow turned into a quagmire, miring this prong of the forward movement in the mud.

Brig. Gen. Thomas J. Wood commanded the leading division of Crittenden's Corps. He later noted, "It has scarcely ever been my misfortune in eighteen years of active service, during which I have marched many thousands of miles, to have to pass over so bad a road. The geological formation of the plateau is such as to make in wet weather the very worst roads conceivable." Although Crittenden had been provided with four companies of Pioneers to repair the road, he still needed fifty men to assist each wagon. In addition, artillery pieces had to be double-teamed and assigned up to fifty men each at the worst spots along the way. Despite the best efforts of men and animals, Crittenden managed to cover twenty-one miles in a five-day period.[5]

Options

Option One

Rosecrans could wait for the weather to break and for the roads to dry enough to allow Crittenden to continue on as the lead element of the advance. Crittenden's assigned route held the best opportunity for reaching and turning Bragg's flank. The drawback of this option was that it gave Bragg time to react to Rosecrans's move. On June 26 Bragg was not fully aware of the disposition of the Union forces, so the initiative still was in Rosecrans's hands.

Option Two

Rosecrans could change assignments, making Thomas's Corps the main strike force while trusting that McCook could cover the eight miles from Liberty Gap to Hoover's Gap in a timely fashion despite the rain and muddy roads. McCook would then be in position to support Thomas. Such a move would leave the Union cavalry in the rear, so all the functions usually carried out by cavalry would devolve on Wilder's mounted infantry. The distance from Hoover's Gap to Manchester was about twelve miles, and a rapid thrust might still gain control of Elk River and sever the Nashville & Chattanooga Railroad.

Decision

Rosecrans chose the second option. Thomas's Corps would take the lead and would advance on Manchester. McCook and the Twentieth Corps would abandon their feint at Liberty Gap and move to join the Fourteenth Corps at Hoover's Gap. Crittenden would have to continue to struggle through the mud as best he could, but the combination of Thomas and McCook at Manchester would give Rosecrans enough force to carry out the general intention of his original plan.

Impact/Resuts

Although Thomas did not move until June 26, Rosecrans retained the initiative in the campaign. The advance on Manchester forced the abandonment of the food-producing area to the west of the main Confederate position. This circumstance, along with the seizure of roads leading to crossings on the Elk River, convinced Bragg to leave both his fortified positions at Shelbyville and Tullahoma. Rosecrans's flexibility in altering his plan to adapt to the changed conditions proved a major contribution to the success of the Tullahoma Campaign.

Bragg Evacuates Shelbyville

Situation

Fighting had begun at Hoover's Gap and at Liberty Gap north and east of Shelbyville on June 24, but Bragg left Polk's Corps in place at Shelbyville for three days. During a day and a half of this period Union cavalry was active to the west and north of Polk's position, but the blue horsemen had fallen back to Christiana during the day on the twenty-fifth. It appeared that Bragg had been deceived by the feint made by the Union cavalry and was hoping that the main attack would come at Shelbyville.

Leonidas Polk.

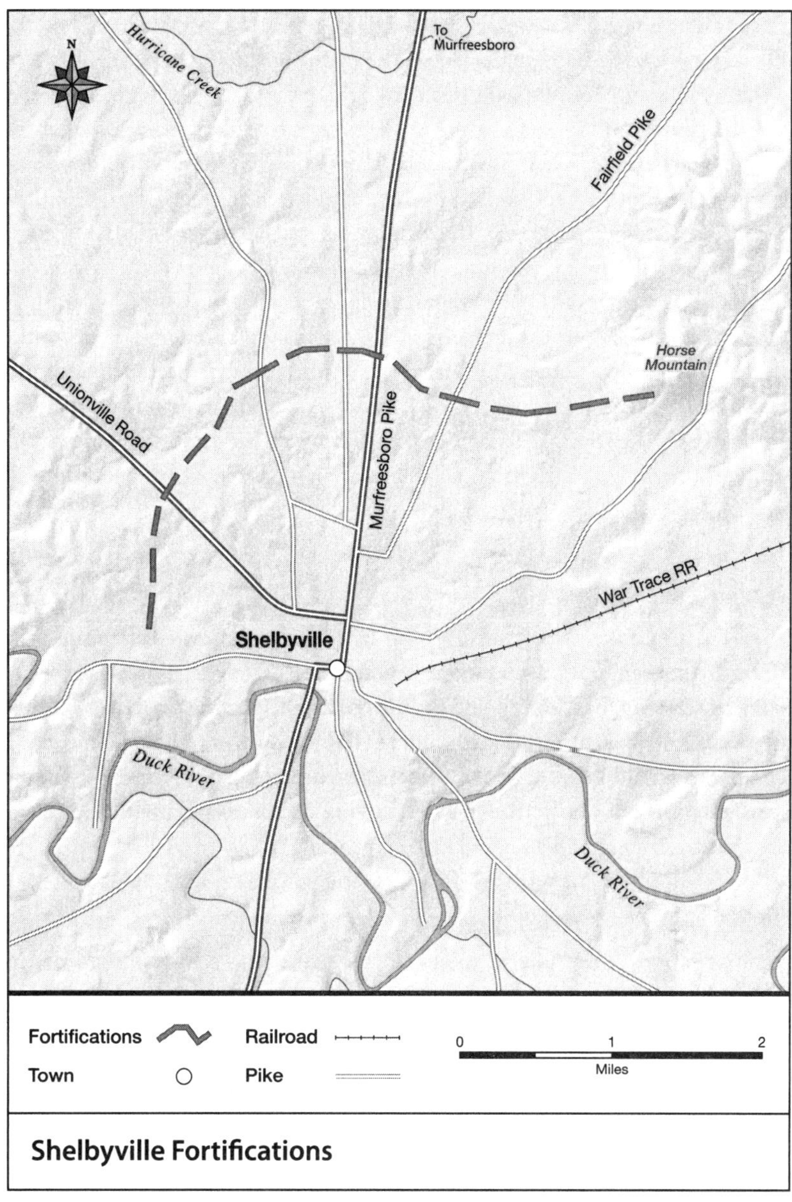

Shelbyville Fortifications

The town of Shelbyville is located in a wide, sweeping bend of the Duck River. Elaborate and extensive fortifications had been erected on the hills and ridges enclosing the town on the western and northern sides. The memory of the Union disaster at Fredericksburg, Virginia, in December 1862 was still fresh, and Bragg was perhaps dreaming of repeating on the banks of the Duck what Lee had accomplished on the banks of the Rappahannock.

June 27 saw McCook pull back from Liberty Gap and begin his move toward Thomas at Hoover's Gap. On the same day, Thomas lashed out at the Confederates under Gen. William B. Bate who were observing the moves of the Fourteenth Corps and began his move toward Manchester. Thomas's move farther toward Bragg's right flank convinced the Confederate commander that the time had come to abandon Shelbyville and to concentrate his forces at Tullahoma. The wagons belonging to Maj. Gen. Benjamin F. Cheatham's division were sent toward Tullahoma via Shofner's Bridge, while those of Maj. Gen. Jones M. Withers's division crossed the Duck at Skullcamp Bridge. The infantry preceded them.[6] A cavalry division commanded by Brig. Gen. William T. Martin, a transfer from the Army of Northern Virginia who was new to division command, remained to cover the withdrawal.

Options

Option One

A basic rule of warfare states, "In the face of the enemy, concentrate your forces." The penetration of Hoover's Gap and the advance on Manchester were reasons for abandoning Shelbyville and concentrating the Army of Tennessee at Tullahoma. This move would avoid the danger of being defeated in detail and would give the Confederates another opportunity to fight from a fortified position. The option to evacuate was also in keeping with the defensive posture Bragg had assumed since January.

Option Two

Concentration in the face of the enemy is a rule that should sometimes be broken. Lee had just disregarded the principle of concentration at Chancellorsville and had won an immense victory. Bragg could make the same choice.

There were no Union infantrymen within fifteen to twenty miles of Shelbyville, and those soldiers were marching farther and farther away. The only Northern force near Polk's Corps was cavalry, and a large, efficient cavalry force under Forrest was stationed to Polk's west. Polk and Forrest could therefore unite and strike north toward Murfreesboro and the rear of the Union position at Hoover's Gap.

Results

Bragg chose Option 1, and a cavalry battle in Shelbyville wrecked Martin's Division.

Alternative Scenario

Could Leonidas Polk have exercised independent command successfully and led an offensive operation with his corps? The strategic situation at Shelbyville offered Polk a chance to attempt such a move, which might have brought the Tullahoma Campaign to quite a different end.

Polk already held Guy's Gap, and his position was not threatened by infantry, only by cavalry approaching his right flank and front. Forrest was able to take the saddle by June 27, and Confederate cavalry had an open route via Unionville to guard the left flank of any movement Polk might make. Polk had the option of advancing toward Fosterville, at which point he could have blocked the route McCook had used to advance from Murfreesboro. Upon reaching Fosterville, Polk could have turned east to attack the right flank of McCook's Corps at Liberty Gap while Cleburne held the Union force in place. If McCook had decided to withdraw in the face of such a move, his only choice would have been traveling country roads northeast to join Thomas at Hoover's Gap. The route back to Murfreesboro was in Confederate hands.

Once in possession of Fosterville the Confederates would have been ten miles in the rear of Thomas at Hoover's Gap and about eight miles from Murfreesboro, so a farther advance on that place would have been conceivable. Fortress Rosecrans was garrisoned by a single brigade and though the strength of the works would have made it difficult to capture, a strong Confederate presence at Murfreesboro would have separated Rosecrans from his base of supplies. Would Rosecrans have been able to ignore the threat to his supply base, or would he have ordered Thomas and McCook to fall back on Murfreesboro? Would the Confederates have ignored the supply base at Murfreesboro and moved against Thomas's rear while Cleburne advanced from Liberty Gap, which Cook had abandoned, to reinforce Polk? Crittenden was several miles away, bogged in the mud, and the same mud meant no wagons were moving out of Murfreesboro to resupply the Union forces at Hoover's Gap. Thomas and McCook could have been cut off from their supply base both by Polk and by the bad roads.

Hardee had his troops in position to move against Hoover's Gap if the opportunity arose, so Rosecrans could conceivably have been forced to fight a united Army of Tennessee with only two of his three corps present and supplies dwindling. If Polk did not feel strong enough to offer battle after reaching Fosterville, threatening both McCook's flank and the supply base at Murfreesboro, he might have held his position for two or three days. He could then have withdrawn toward Shelbyville via Guy's Gap or toward Tullahoma via Liberty Gap and Wartrace. Either of these moves could have negatively affected Rosecrans's plan. The passage of the additional time would have used up his available provisions to the extent that he might have had to fall back to Murfreesboro to resupply his army.

Rosecrans Does Not Pause at Manchester but Continues to Maneuver

Situation

Rosecrans had turned the right flank of the Confederate position with a minimum loss of life, although Crittenden's Corps was out of the picture for the moment, being bogged in the mud near the community of Pocahontas. McCook had abandoned his feint at Liberty Gap and was closing up on Thomas, who was marching on Manchester.[7] From Manchester one road led east and southeast to the village of Pelham and then up the Cumberland Plateau to Monteagle. At that village it intersected the main road, which Bragg would use if he withdrew to Chattanooga. Another road led west and southwest to Tullahoma, where the Army of Tennessee was in the process of concentrating. Also at Tullahoma, yet another road branched off from the Pelham route to turn south toward Decherd, a station on the Nashville & Chattanooga Railroad along which Bragg's supplies flowed.

Rosecrans had achieved a very important objective and now could potentially trap the Army of Tennessee. One of the problems to be considered was that his forces were somewhat scattered while Bragg's had the opportunity to reunite before the Army of the Cumberland could do so. Then there was the matter of supplies. The Northern men had left Murfreesboro with three days' rations in their haversacks and another seven days' worth in the wagons accompanying them. These rations were about half used up, and the condition of the roads did not allow wagons to reach the army with a resupply. The population of the area was too sparse to allow the army to subsist by foraging; indeed, Rosecrans's location was known as "the barrens."[8]

Options

Option One

With the Army of Tennessee "in the bag" Rosecrans had accomplished a great deal. But did he have the manpower and supplies to "tie shut the mouth of the bag"?

One option was to pause at Manchester long enough for Crittenden to join the rest of the army, and for McCook to complete his move from Liberty Gap. The problem of supplies would take longer to solve because wagons

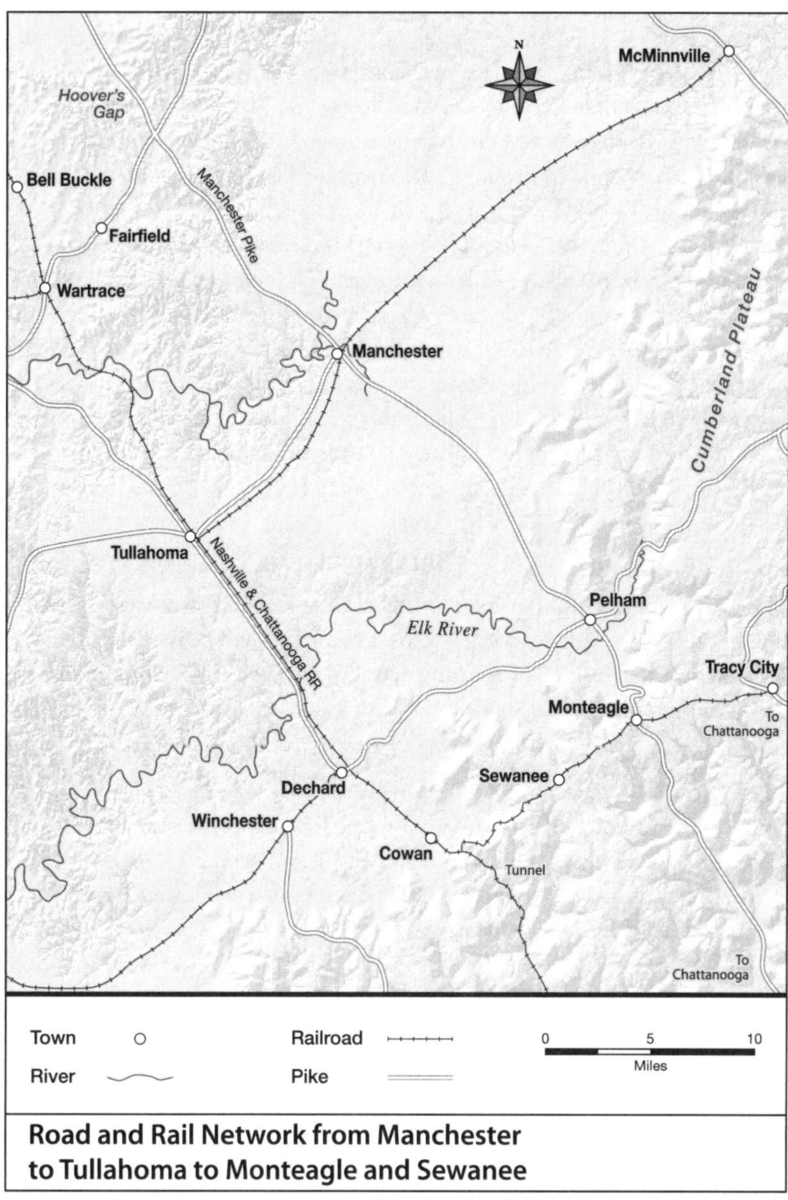

Road and Rail Network from Manchester to Tullahoma to Monteagle and Sewanee

could not move forward from Murfreesboro until the roads dried. The need to reunite forces and to resupply the army were cogent arguments in favor of a delay at Manchester. The obvious negative factor was that a delay would give Bragg time to think and to react.

Option Two

Rosecrans could send his only available mounted force, Wilder's Brigade, to Pelham and then south to Decherd to hit the Nashville & Chattanooga Railroad. This course of action would annoy Bragg and divert his troops' attention away from confronting the Army of the Cumberland and toward protecting his supply line.

While the mounted infantry was on the move the rest of the available forces could advance some six miles toward Tullahoma, where the hills bordering Compton's Creek provided a good position. Additionally, an advance to the creek would leave Rosecrans in control of two additional roads leading southeast to Elk River. Union troops would then have an additional opportunity to force Bragg to fight at a disadvantage.

The shortage of supplies and the scattered position of Crittenden and McCook argued against this option.

Decision

Rosecrans chose Option 2 because it held the possibility of destroying his enemy and of winning a decisive victory. Rosecrans had begin the Tullahoma Campaign with the goal of winning decisively, and he chose to continue opearting in that fashion on June 28.

Results

Wilder managed to inflict only minor damage on the railroad at Decherd, but even this distracted Bragg and caused him to send a brigade of cavalry to pursue Wilder. The absence of Confederate cavalry allowed Rosecrans to advance to the hills along Compton's Creek and to seize control of two roads leading to the Elk River. These results forced Bragg to reconsider his options relative to his position at Tullahoma.

Alternative Scenario

Rosecrans might have been emboldened to chose Option 1 since Bragg showed no signs of abandoning his defensive strategy. When the Army of the Cumberland had concentrated, Rosecrans could have sent one corps toward Tullahoma to attract and hold Bragg's attention while sending the rest of his force up the Cumberland Plateau via the village of Pelham. Wilder had already found this route unguarded as far as the Elk River at Pelham.

At the top of the plateau Rosecrans would be in a blocking position on the best route to Chattanooga via Tracy City, the route eventually followed by Hardee's Corps. An advance of seven miles to University Station would have blocked the remaining practical route to Chattanooga, the one eventually followed by Polk's Corps. A pause to concentrate his forces might have allowed Rosecrans to trap and destroy the Army of Tennessee.

Bragg Evacuates Tullahoma

Situation

Bragg's cavalry brought him the news that the Army of the Cumberland was concentrating along Compton's Creek, about six miles toward Manchester. Bragg responded as expected by ordering some infantry and most of his cavalry forward to confront this move. As skirmishing developed along the low hills bordering the creek, most of the Confederate infantry was engaged in completing the fortifications around Tullahoma. Some substantial fortifications had been constructed to protect Bragg's supply depot. Fort Rains, named for Gen. James Edward Rains, who was killed in action at Murfreesboro, could hold a garrison of five hundred men and twelve cannon. Breastworks and gun emplacements had been thrown up for several hundred yards on either side of this earthwork, but there were gaps in the works, and these were now hastily addressed.[9] While this work was in progress, Wilder made his raid on the Nashville & Chattanooga at Decherd, drawing attention to the vulnerable state of the Confederate supply line.

On June 28 Bragg had called a council of war with his corps commanders to address the Army of the Cumberland's developing advance. The officers decided to make a stand at Tullahoma.[10] June 30 saw Bragg call a second council, and this time he faced opposition from Polk and Hardee. Polk wanted to know how the line of supply for the army was to be protected, since there was not enough cavalry to cover the front and flanks of the infantry and guard the rail line. Hardee feared that the army would be surrounded in thirty-six hours and forced to surrender. He pointed out that the flat terrain around Tullahoma did not provide any location where the army could anchor the flanks of its lines.

Options

Option One

Polk and Hardee both presented cogent arguments favoring evacuation of Tullahoma. The once-mighty Confederate cavalry force available to Bragg had been seriously diminished through troops' dispersement to Mississippi, Morgan's disobedience to orders, and Wheeler's and Martin's decisive defeat at Shelbyville on June 29. Forrest, with one brigade, was the largest unit of cavalry Bragg still had at his command. If battle was accepted at Tullahoma and the

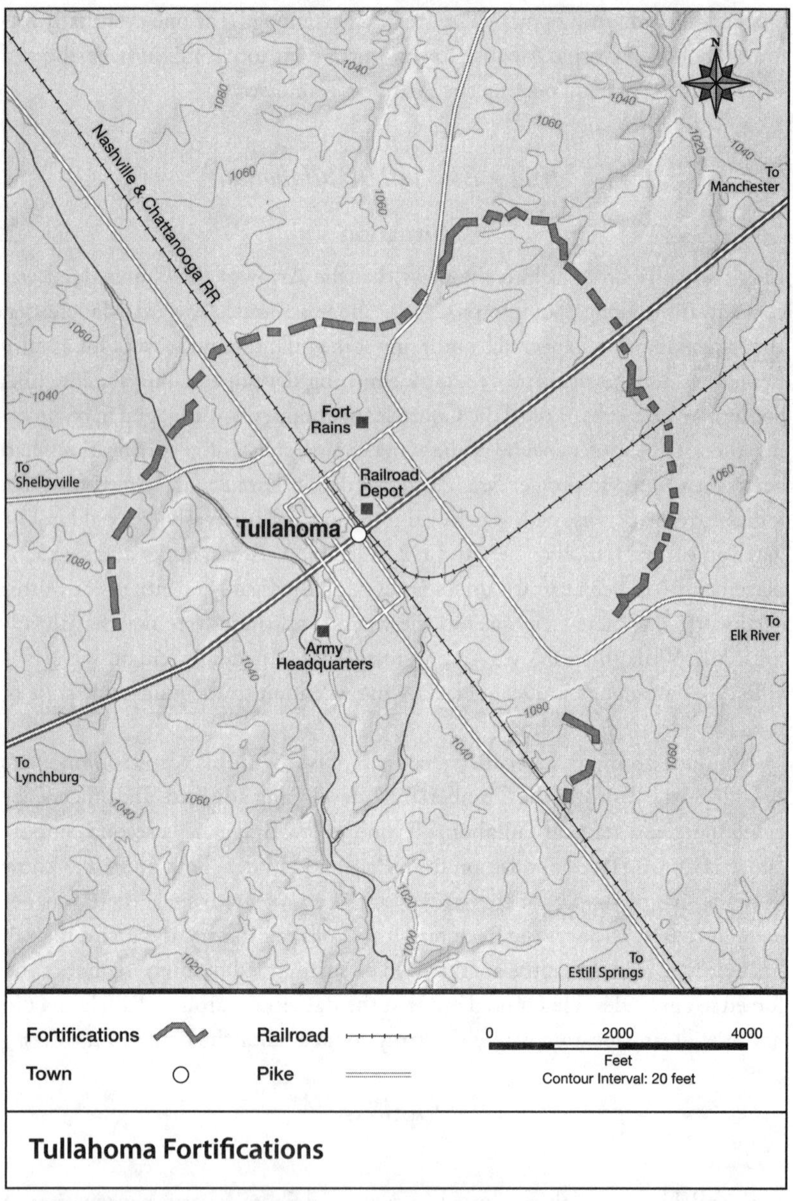

Tullahoma Fortifications

Army of Tennessee was defeated, the route to Chattanooga would surely be closed. The only available line of retreat would lie to the south, across the Tennessee River and into the Sand Mountain region of Alabama, an area of sparse population and poor soil. The army was not likely to retain its cohesion there.

These weighty reasons deserved careful consideration.

Option Two

Nothing of significance had changed since June 28, when Bragg and his corps commanders had agreed to stand and fight. The fortifications at Tullahoma had been strengthened, and Bragg had sufficient rations on-site to feed his men for a week or more. If the rail line supplying his army was cut for a short time, no real harm would be done. A battle was risky, but Bragg had his army concentrated while the Army of the Cumberland was still lacking one corps, Crittenden's.

The key factor for the second option was food. Bragg had several days' worth of food, and Rosecrans had three days' worth of supplies. Had Bragg known this—and good cavalry work should have supplied him with this intelligence—fighting at Tullahoma offered a good chance for success. General Hunger would fight on the side of the South. When Federal forces occupied Tullahoma on July 1, they discovered 1,200 pounds of hardtack left behind by the Confederates and immediately issued it to the Union troops, who were out of rations.

Results

General Bragg had been on the defensive for the last six months. He could not bring himself to change his stance, so evacuation was decided on. As a result of the council of war, Hardee's wagon train began to leave town via the Bethpage Road, while Polk's took the Winchester Road via Winchester Springs. By five o'clock on the morning of July 1 most of the infantry was across Elk River.[11]

Alternative Scenario

At the June 30 council of war Bragg could have rejected the advice of Hardee and Polk and ordered the defense of Tullahoma. On July 1 skirmishing and rearguard activity reasonably could have limited the Army of the Cumberland to an advance of six miles from Compton's Creek to the fortified lines at Tullahoma. Rosecrans might have used the available roads from the Compton's Creek area to move forces toward Elk River, but these forces would have found their crossings opposed by Confederate cavalry. This blocking force, and the flooded river, arguably would have prevented a crossing.

On July 2 the Union force might have assaulted the Confederate lines blocking the Army of the Cumberland's approach from Manchester. In the sector facing the Union advance the lines were strong, and the Confederate defense had a very reasonable chance to repel the attack. Such a repulse could produce a stalemate while Rosecrans sought an alternative solution.

July 3 would see the commissary wagons of the Army of the Cumberland emptied. Behind the Army of the Cumberland a two-and-one-half mile gap

William J. Hardee.

in the rail tracks leading to Murfreesboro remained. Also, a bridge over Duck River had been destroyed during the Confederate retreat from Liberty Gap, and a ninety-foot-long trestle needed to be rebuilt at Normandy. Rosecrans had been notified that a train of wagons was on its way from Murfreesboro, but the dispatch containing this news also informed him, "Heaven knows when it may reach you owing to the bad state of the roads." This meant that while Bragg's line of supplies was threatened, Rosecrans had no line of supply operating at all and was out of food.[12]

July 4 saw Lee begin his retreat from Gettysburg and Grant enter Vicksburg. It might also have seen Rosecrans begin a hungry march toward Murfreesboro, harried by Confederate cavalry and pursued by infantry.

Bragg Abandons Middle Tennessee

Situation

The close of day on July 1 found Bragg's army safely across Elk River. The flooded river limited the crossings available, and Bragg took up positions to cover them in order to confront the pursuit he was certain Rosecrans would mount.

Daybreak on July 2 found Confederate cavalry blocking the Morris Ferry crossing with Cheatham's Division downstream at Bethpage Bridge. Slightly farther downstream, Withers's Division occupied the railroad bridge at Estill Springs (also called Alisonia), while Hardee's Corps formed a reserve in the rear in the direction of Winchester. The left flank was posted at a ford crossing Elk River at Rock Creek. The terrain on the left bank of the Elk afforded good defensive positions for the Confederates.[13]

Though Rosecrans's logistics situation had become even more intense with the passing of another two days, Bragg remained unaware of this fact and showed no intention of fighting along the line of the Elk. During July 2 the Confederate forces abandoned their positions along Elk River and fell back to Cowan, a village at the very foot of the Cumberland Plateau. During the day of July 3, as Union forces converged on their position and threatened to outflank them on their right, Bragg decided to abandon Middle Tennessee and ordered the army to move toward Chattanooga.[14]

On July 4 Union and Confederate troops fought a skirmish atop the Cumberland Plateau at University Station, today called Sewanee, the site of the University of the South, which Bishop Leonidas Polk had founded prior to the war. Polk, now a lieutenant general, paused briefly on the campus as his troops retreated along the road to Chattanooga.[15]

Options

Option One

The Elk River line was a good defensive position, at least so long as the river remained at flood stage. Bragg had the option of offering battle from positions along the left bank of the river, and even if Rosecrans refused battle, a stand along the Elk would delay the Union advance. Although Bragg might not have been aware of the Union forces' state of supplies, a stand of two or three days along the Elk would have serious consequences for Rosecrans.

Option Two

Polk and Hardee exchanged letters on July 2 in which they discussed the possibility of declaring Bragg unfit for duty and replacing him with either of themselves. Whether this change in command would have made a difference is open to question, but the two seemed somewhat more belligerent than Bragg, although their advice had led to abandoning Tullahoma.

Results

The decision to abandon Middle Tennessee without a fight cemented the accomplishment of Rosecrans's army and gave the validation of success to his plan of campaign. The results of Bragg's decision opened the way for the Union advance on Chattanooga, set up the circumstances leading to the Battle of Chickamauga, and shifted the starting point of the Atlanta Campaign of 1864 from Middle Tennessee to north Georgia.

As argued in the preface to this book, the results of the Tullahoma Campaign were of greater strategic importance to the Union cause than either Vicksburg or Gettysburg.

Alternative Scenario

Option 1 offered the possibility for an alternative result for the Tullahoma Campaign. Holding a defensive position behind a flooded river would have been an easy and sound military decision, even if the army commander had further retreat in mind. Had Bragg held his position along the Elk for another two days, until July 4, Rosecrans would have been reduced to foraging for food in the surrounding area. As has been stated, the area around Tullahoma was (and is) called "the barrens"—no food was available. A defensive stand by Bragg along the Elk would have seen Rosecrans facing a very difficult logistical situation.

NOTE: Rosecrans did begin foraging for food on July 4, but by moving across the Elk River he had been able to occupy an area richer in agricultural produce.

CHAPTER 3

AFTERMATH OF THE CAMPAIGN

By July 6 the Army of Tennessee was concentrating in and around Chattanooga. At the same time, desertion had become a problem in those regiments raised in Middle Tennessee. Men were returning home to attempt to protect their families from Union soldiers who formed foraging parties, guerrillas who were already becoming endemic in the area, and gangs of outlaws including Union and Confederate deserters, as well as a few former slaves who seized the opportunity to free themselves and extract a measure of revenge for their enslavement.[1]

Rosecrans anticipated trouble if the civilian population was abused, and he moved to counter such actions. On July 6 he sent out a circular noting that Union troops were committing severe depredations on civilians. Soldiers were ordered to stop the plunder and pay for the damages. July 9 saw an order issued to Major General Sheridan to control his troops and to enforce discipline. The directive read, "Disloyalty does not forfeit the rights of humanity which every true soldier will respect." Special Order 101 was issued on August 13, and it established a Board of Appraisers to assess the damages sustained by citizens of Franklin County and to arrange reimbursement. Chief of Staff Garfield summed up the situation in a letter to General Stanley, who commanded the cavalry: "The lawlessness of our soldiers on foraging parties will make bushwhackers faster than any other thing." Garfield was prophetic. The Cumberland Plateau soon became infested with guerrillas and remained so to the end of the war.[2]

Despite his fearsome reputation as a general who shot deserters, Bragg adopted a more conciliatory attitude on this occasion, offering to allow men to return to the ranks with some degree of leniency. However, Bragg took no steps to reconcile himself with his subordinate officers or to create a leadership team.[3]

The Army of the Cumberland spread itself along the valley of the Elk River and posted detachments atop the Cumberland Plateau. While the men rested and dried out from the heavy rains of the previous ten days, Rosecrans concentrated on rebuilding the Nashville & Chattanooga Railroad to reconnect his army with its base of supply at Murfreesboro. Collecting Confederate deserters, fending off guerrillas, and dealing with the War Department in Washington took up a great deal of time.[4]

Rosecrans Pauses to Refit and Resupply

Situation

Rosecrans was at the end of his supplies, but behind him were an inoperable railroad and forty miles of roads that were no better than a quagmire. Having spent the last ten days wet through from heavy rains, the men were tired, the horses and mules exhausted. A degree of disorganization was inevitable.

The Union forces established strong outposts atop the Cumberland Plateau at University Place (now called Sewanee) and at Tracy City from which to watch the roads toward Chattanooga and then spread themselves over the

Edwin Stanton.

farms and fields at the foot of the plateau. Headquarters was established at Winchester, Tennessee, and divisions were placed at Cowan, Decherd, Estill Springs, and Tullahoma along the railroad.

Despite the obvious need to rectify the supply situation, Washington officials pressured Union forces to stay on the move. Secretary of War Edwin Stanton remarked in a telegram to Rosecrans, "You and your noble army now have the chance to give the finishing blow to the rebellion. Will you neglect the chance?" This message must have felt like a bucket of icy water dumped over the head of the commanding general of the Army of the Cumberland. In ten days he had advanced almost fifty miles with only minor casualties and had driven his opponent out of the valuable Middle Tennessee area. Given the numerous telegrams Rosecrans sent to Stanton reporting his advances and occupation of territory, the general had every reason to assume the secretary of war was aware of the Army of the Cumberland's actions. Rosecrans replied to Stanton, "You do not appear to observe the fact that this noble army has driven the rebels from Middle Tennessee, of which my dispatches advised you. I beg in behalf of this army that the War Department may not overlook so great an event because it is not written in letters of blood."[5]

Options

Option One

Rosecrans understood very well the lack of food in his command. He was also quite aware that the Cumberland Plateau was even more devoid of foodstuffs than was the Oak Barrens, through which he had just passed. The Nashville & Chattanooga Railroad would be repaired within a week to ten days, and supplies would flow down the tracks from Fortress Rosecrans. It was reasonable to assume that the unusual weather pattern of heavy rain would end and the roads would become passable. As events proved, it was six weeks before Rosecrans was adequately supplied. Even so, all these arguments made pausing to refit and resupply a reasonable option.

Option Two

Stanton's telegram showed quite plainly that the friction between the two men that had evidenced itself during the long pause at Murfreesboro was not gone. Federal troops had already paused for 169 days, and Stanton did not seem to consider a ten-day campaign sufficient justification for another pause.

Rosecrans could send a division or two toward Chattanooga to probe the Confederate position, thereby offering some satisfaction to Stanton and protecting his own standing with the War Department. Such a move would entail risk since the entire Army of Tennessee might concentrate against such a probe and defeat it. But taking the risk would offer Rosecrans some personal protection with Washington.

Decision

Rosecrans decided to wait for the railroad to be repaired and for the roads to dry. He placed the welfare of his men and the safety of his army above his personal standing with the War Department.

Result

Rosecrans was able to refit his men and to resupply his army. His attention to protecting the Nashville & Chattanooga Railroad allowed the rails to be opened as far as the Tennessee River and, eventually, to Chattanooga. The Army of the Cumberland would continue its advance within six weeks.

As Rosecrans expected, the pause to refit and resupply exacerbated his strained relations with the War Department. Assistant Secretary of War Charles Dana was sent to act as a supervisor and "snitch," keeping an eye on the operations of the army.

Bragg Opts to Remain On the Defensive

Situation

The Army of Tennessee was safely ensconced in and around Chattanooga. The losses in men and equipment during the Tullahoma Campaign had been small, and most of the men continued to exhibit high morale. At the same time, those whose homes had just come under Union occupation showed signs of worry. Desertion from the ranks of units from the recently occupied areas was higher than average for the army as a whole.

Chattanooga was a strong position for the Confederates, as the East Tennessee & Virginia Railroad linked it to Richmond, and the Western & Atlantic linked it to Atlanta. This rail connection provided an opportunity for the easy flow of reinforcements from north and south while being only a short distance from the major supply base of Atlanta.

The mountains surrounding Chattanooga for some distance on all sides provided excellent terrain for defense, as long as an active cavalry force supplied accurate intelligence of enemy movements. Bragg found the effectiveness of his mounted arm becoming less certain. For the first time in their history, Bragg's men faced opposition from a large part of the civilian population. Chattanooga had favored secession, but the surrounding rural areas had

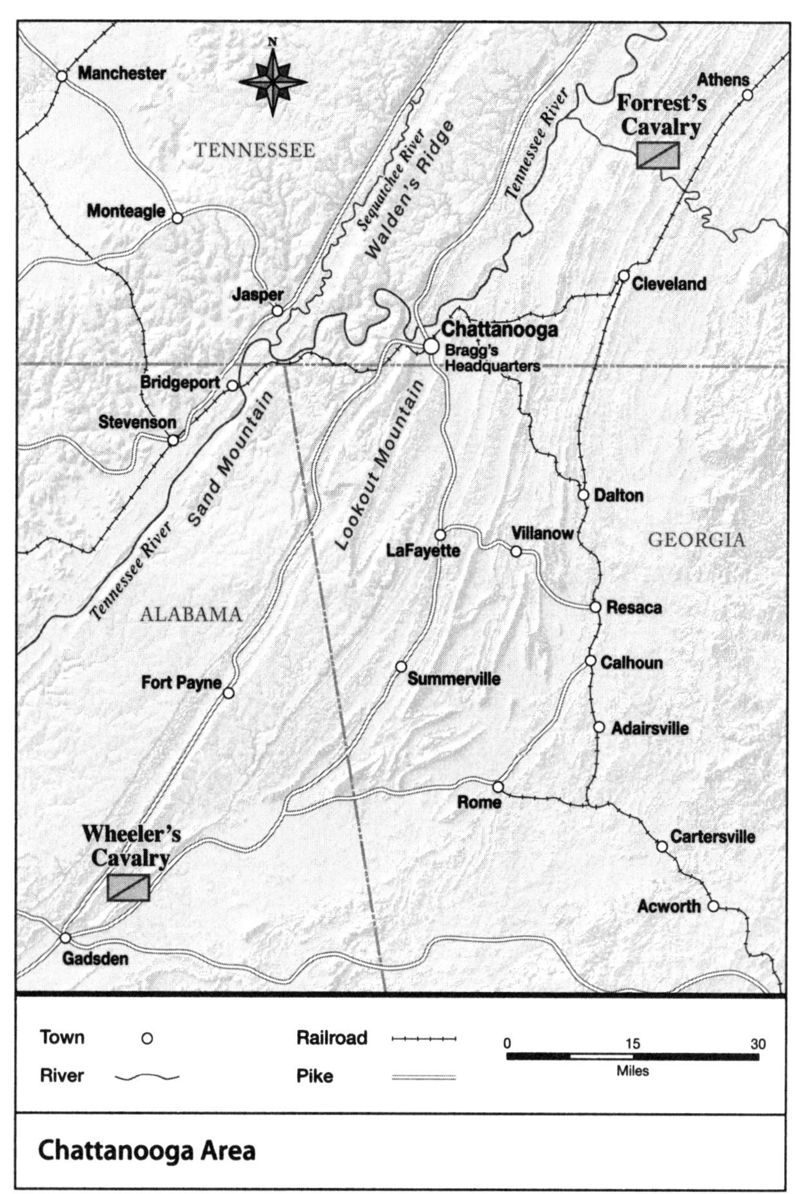

Chattanooga Area

Simon Bolivar Buckner.

voted to stay with the Union. The meaning of "civil war" was about to become clear for the Tennesseans.[6]

Bragg continued to have difficulty in securing his subordinate officers' cooperation, and several changes in command took place. Hardee left to join Johnston in Mississippi, while Maj. Gen. Daniel Harvey Hill came to join the Army of Tennessee. Maj. Gen. Simon Bolivar Buckner also came under Bragg's command, and the two men did not get along well.[7]

As he saw no sign of Rosecrans, Bragg had to decide how to use his army.

Options

Option One

The Confederate cavalry, once the strongest element of Bragg's force, could be sent onto the Cumberland Plateau. Ranging over the mountains and basing themselves in the Sequatchie Valley, the horsemen would be in position to harass the Army of the Cumberland's attempts to refit and resupply while opposing every move the Union forces made onto the plateau. Contesting the ground from the valley of the Elk River to the environs of Chattanooga would buy time for Bragg to secure reinforcements. It might also provide him an opportunity to strike his enemy in detail as the elements of the Union force moved across the plateau.

Option Two

Bragg could continue the defensive policy he had followed ever since the

Battle of Stones River. That policy had proven to be a disastrous failure in the Tullahoma Campaign, but given Bragg's lack of confidence in his cavalry and his squabbles with his subordinate commanders, remaining on the defensive was easier.

Decision

Bragg chose to remain on the defensive. Wheeler's troopers were allowed to go to Gadsden, Alabama, where they were completely out of position to oppose any Union move across the Cumberland Plateau. Forrest's command was sent up the Tennessee River, north of Chattanooga, to guard the crossings of the river in case Rosecrans decided to strike for the area between Chattanooga and Knoxville.

Results

The results of Bragg's decision were conceding to Rosecrans all the territory between the Elk River and Chattanooga and allowing time and tranquility in which the Army of the Cumberland could prepare for its next move. This passive attitude only fueled the discontent of Bragg's subordinates. It also led the Confederate War Department to question Bragg as to what he was going to do with the men if he received reinforcements.

Conclusion

The results of the Tullahoma Campaign brought the Union much closer to final victory; thus the campaign is more important than most historians recognize. Rosecrans took control of Middle Tennessee and its food-producing capacity, manufacturers, transportation net, and pool of recruits. These are the actions any commanding general must take to win wars. The critical decisions by which Rosecrans achieved these goals are worthy of study.

Lessons Learned from the Tullahoma Campaign

John Wilder's brigade of mounted infantry proved the value of the Spencer repeater at Hoover's Gap and again at Decherd. This lesson made Wilder place confidence in the ability of his men to use firepower, not in the ability of numbers of personnel to hold a position. He applied this lesson to advantage at Chickamauga.

The Tullahoma Campaign demonstrated the changing nature of war. Instead of the old concept of winning by destroying the opposing army, Tullahoma helped introduce the modern concept of occupying territory and depriving the enemy of infrastructure. Some military leaders' and many civilian leaders' continued fascination with fighting battles of annihilation prevented this fact from being recognized as it might have been.

The Tullahoma Campaign was the highest achievement of William S. Rosecrans. His ability as a strategic thinker, organizer, and commander classes him among the leading generals produced by the United States Army. The defeat at Chickamauga and Rosecrans's personal disagreement with Ulysses Grant have caused his accomplishments in the Tullahoma Campaign to be overlooked.

APPENDIX I

DRIVING TOUR FOR THE CRITICAL DECISIONS OF THE TULLAHOMA CAMPAIGN

This tour begins in Murfreesboro, headquarters of the Army of the Cumberland from January until late June 1863, and it leads to many, though not all, of the important sites in the development of the Tullahoma Campaign. As much as possible, you will avoid using Interstate 24, which is today the major traffic artery between Murfreesboro and Chattanooga. Instead, this tour utilizes older US highways, state highways, and county roads. All these routes are clearly marked and signposted, so there should be no difficulty in following the directions. Using secondary roads, many of which closely follow the 1863 road network, allows those taking this tour to gain an appreciation for the terrain of the Highland Rim and to visualize the influence the terrain exercised on the campaign. The trip begins in Murfreesboro and ends at Sewanee since both armies moved in that direction during the campaign. The stops are arranged in chronological order, but some of them will deal with simultaneous events. Many of the critical decisions of the Tullahoma Campaign were made before actual movement of troops began, and a specific location cannot be assigned to these decisions.

Stop 1—Fortress Rosecrans, the Secure Base of Supplies

From downtown Murfreesboro follow US 41 north to the intersection with State Route (SR) 96, which is also signposted "Old Fort Parkway." Turn west toward Interstate 24 on SR 96. SR 96 intersects I-24, and Fortress Rosecrans may be reached from the interstate by following SR 96 toward downtown Murfreesboro.

Approximately 0.50 mile from the intersection of SR 96 and US 41, turn into Old Fort Park on the north side of the road. Follow the park road through the picnic area, playground, and ball fields until you reach the parking area for Fortress Rosecrans, which is clearly signposted.

Park and take the walking trail leading into Fortress Rosecrans. Notice the numerous interpretative signs along the paved walkway. When you have finished exploring the interior of the fort, return to your car.

Hard Times in Occupied Murfreesboro

John Spence, a civilian resident of Murfreesboro, kept a diary in which he described life in the occupied city. He stated in one entry, "The Presbyterian Church, a two story building forty by sixty feet, has been demolished. It was used as a hospital for both Confederates and Federals following the battle, but when the wounded had all be evacuated, it was turned into a stable for the Yankee cavalry. Now all the pews and other wood have been taken away and smashed up for firewood and the building is being demolished and the bricks used to build bake ovens in the fort being built outside town." By the end of March 1864 Spence noted, "All the timber for miles around has been destroyed, all the fence rails burned for three or four miles in all directions, and at least 50 houses have been torn down so the military can use their materials. Even the fence around the cemetery has been torn down."[1]

Stop 2—Hoover's Gap

Leaving Fortress Rosecrans, return to the park entrance. Turn right onto SR 96 and proceed 1.50 miles to I-24, Exit 78. Take I-24 East toward Chattanooga. At Exit 89, exit right onto Epps Mill Road. Turn left on Epps Mill, and cross over I-24. Proceed to the end of Epps Mill Road at a T-intersection with US 41, then turn right (south) on US 41. You are now following the route Wilder's Brigade used to approach Hoover's Gap on June 24. A few yards left of US 41, you will occasionally see traces of the 1863 roadbed.

Shortly after turning onto US 41, the road ascends the shoulder of a hill. This hill was the location of a Confederate observation post in 1863, but because of limited visibility due to rain, it was not manned on June 24. Looking from your left, across your front, and around to your right you can see the hills that form the Highland Rim. Ahead of you can be seen the open land of Hoover's Gap. The hills on either side of you as you enter the gap are three hundred to four hundred feet higher than the elevation of the road.

At the sign marked "Beech Grove" look for a fork to the right. Take this road. This is the original 1863 road. The Beech Grove cemetery appears immediately on your right behind two houses. Watch for a sharp right turn on a road posted "Confederate Cemetery." Follow this road into the cemetery, and park in the paved area. The location of the critical decision to adopt repeating weapons is unknown, but you are now at the site of the decision's implementation in combat.

The cemetery marks the left flank of Wilder's position. Two companies of the Ninety-Second Illinois were positioned across the 1863 road on which you entered, and the Seventy-Second Indiana was "refused" along the ridge on which the cemetery is located. A replica of a three-inch ordnance rifle marks the spot where Eli Lilly located two guns of his battery, and the rest of Wilder's line stretched at an angle to the right of the fieldpiece, crossing the route of present-day I-24. A cell-phone tower marks the approximate right flank of Wilder's line.

The Confederate position, occupied by Brig. Gen. William Brimage Bate's brigade, was to your front as you stand at the muzzle of the fieldpiece replica. The position where Lilly placed six of his guns, supported by the 123rd Illinois, and where the Twentieth Tennessee attacked, is in the middle of the present interstate. The "conical hill" occupied by Lilly was destroyed by highway construction, becoming the fill raising the roadbed for the present highway bridge over SR 64.

From the Report of General Bate

When about a mile from Beech Grove (which is near the entrance to Hoover's Gap), I threw out a company of skirmishers to my right, and sent forward with a few scouts at his own insistence, Major William Clare, of General Bragg's staff, to ascertain the whereabouts of the enemy. His fire was soon drawn and his position developed. . . . I ordered Col. A. F. Rudler, with the 27th Georgia Regiment, to move his command across the creek up the steep acclivity of its left bank, form line parallel with the same, and give an enfilading fire to the force then heavily engaging my left. The order was

> obeyed with alacrity and in good style. The enemy, anticipating the move, met it with a line of battle fronting the woods which skirted the bank of the creek. A bloody engagement here ensued with great odds against us. . . . In this position we fought for nearly an hour when the enemy, by excess of numbers, turned our already extended left, giving an enfilading fire to the 20th Tennessee. It recoiled from the shock, was rallied, and formed in good time on a fence running a short distance from and perpendicular to our line of battle.[2]

Several markers and interpretative kiosks in the park explain the development of the Tullahoma Campaign and the engagement at Hoover's Gap, also including information about the Spencer rifle.

Civilian graves are located here because this was the community cemetery until 1887. The graves of sixty-four unknown Confederates killed in the fighting here in 1863 are also located in the old community cemetery. Area residents removed their bodies to the graveyard in the days after the battle. The Union dead were removed to Stones River National Cemetery between 1865 and 1867.

A large marker facing the 1863 road is engraved with Nathan Bedford Forrest's May 1865 farewell address to his command, May 1865. There is no historical reason for the presence of this marker in Hoover's Gap; Forrest was never at this location at any time during the war.

Death of Cpl. Christopher McReynolds, Company H, Seventeenth Indiana

> Corporal McReynolds was shot through the breast at the first fire. He had always said the enemy would never get hold of his "Spencer." He hadn't the strength to break it so he took out his knife and unscrewed a part of the lock plate and threw it away, rendering the gun entirely useless. He then fell back amid the storm of bullets, lay down and died.[3]

Stop 3—Bell Buckle

Upon leaving the cemetery turn right and then immediately right again on SR 64, passing under I-24. Proceed 1.70 miles to an intersection signposted

SR 82. Turn right (west) to Bell Buckle, the center of which you will reach in 6.00 miles.

Bell Buckle was the encampment of St. John Liddell's brigade with forward positions at Liberty Gap. Just before crossing the railroad tracks turn sharply right (north) on Main Street, and follow SR 269, which becomes Liberty Pike.

Review of Confederate Troops at Bell Buckle

1st June (Monday) We all went to a review of General Liddell's brigade at Bellbuckle. . . . General Liddell's brigade was composed of Arkansas troops—five very weak regiments which had suffered severely in the different battles, and they cannot be easily recruited on account of the blockade of the Mississippi. The men were good-sized, healthy, and well clothed, though without any attempt at uniformity in color or cut; but nearly all were dressed in gray or brown coats and felt hats.

I was told that even if a regiment was clothed in proper uniform by the government, it would become parti-colored again in a week, as the soldiers preferred wearing the coarse homespun jackets and trousers made by their mothers or sisters at home. The generals very wisely allowed them to please themselves in this respect, and insist only upon their arms and accoutrements being kept in proper order. Most of the officers were dressed in uniform which is neat and servicable—a bluish-gray frock coat of a color similar to Austrian yagers. The infantry wear blue facings, the artillery red, the doctors black, the staff white, and the cavalry yellow; so it is impossible to mistake the branch of service to which an officer belongs—nor is it impossible to mistake his rank. A second lieutenant, first lieutenant, and captain wear respectively one, two, and three bars on the collar. A major, lieutenant colonel, and colonel wear one, two, and three stars on the collar.

Before the marching past of the brigade, many of the soldiers had taken off their coats and marched past the general in their shirt sleeves, on account of the warmth. Most of them were armed with Enfield rifles captured from the enemy. Many, however, had thrown away their bayonets, which they don't appear to value properly, as they assert they have never met any Yankees who would wait for that weapon.

> Each regiment carried a "battle flag," blue, with a white border, on which were inscribed the names "Belmont," "Shiloh," "Perryville," "Richmond, Kentucky," and "Murfreesboro." They drilled tolerably well, and an advance in line was remarkably good.[4]

This account is the only firsthand contemporary description of Confederate troops from the entire war. Lieutenant Colonel Fremantle neglected to note that the "battle flag" had a white disk in the center. This was the flag used by troops belonging to Hardee's Corps from 1862 to 1864. The Army of Tennessee did not use the St. Andrew's cross–pattern battle flag until the Atlanta Campaign.

Stop 4—Liberty Gap

Proceed north on Liberty Pike, signposted as SR 269, until you pass through the gap, a distance of 5.40 miles from Bell Buckle. Unlike Hoover's Gap, Liberty Gap is obviously a gap in the traditional meaning. As you exit the gap note the road turning left at a ninety-degree angle. This is the route of the 1863 road, and it leads to Fosterville and thence to Christiana and Murfreesboro. McCook's lead element traveled this road on June 24. Just past the Fosterville road you will see a road going to the right that is signposted Short Creek Loop. Park on the shoulder of this road.

IMPORTANT NOTE: While there is no good place to park here, there is seldom any traffic on the Short Creek Loop. Carefully walk back to the road used to pass through Liberty Gap, watching for traffic at all times. Face the gap. You are looking at the position held by the advance guard of Liddell's Brigade—540 men of the Fifth Arkansas, Sixth/Seventh Consolidated Arkansas, and Thirteenth/Fifteenth Consolidated Arkansas commanded by Col. Lucius Featherston.[5] Facing the Arkansans was the division of Brig. Gen. R. W. Johnson with Brig. Gen. August Willich commanding the leading brigade. Contemporary descriptions of the area tell us that in 1863 the land was mostly cleared, with the more level land planted in wheat and the hillsides used as pasture. The hills were wooded toward their tops.

Colonel Featherston's men mounted a stiff defense that forced Willich to call for help from the brigade led by Col. Philemon P. Baldwin. These two brigades outflanked Featherston's line, and the Confederates withdrew to the south end of the gap about sundown.

Report of Col. Philemon P. Baldwin, Twenty-Sixth Indiana, Commanding Third Brigade, McCook's Corps

The enemy's position was on a chain of hills, 400 yards distant. The road on reaching their base turned square to the left and followed along their base for 500 yards, to where the hills extend across the road, forming a very strong position, their main force being at the point where the road enters the ills, and this point two pieces of artillery were posted, having a direct fire on part of my line and an enfilading fire on the extreme right until my right occupied the hill held by their left.

At a few minutes after 4 o'clock I put my line in motion. Colonel Berry's regiment gallantly moved forward over the open field on the fight of the road and drove the enemy's skirmishers left from the hills in his front after severe skirmishing, loving 2 killed and 8 wounded and holding the position.

The 6th Indiana moved forward and, on reaching the bend in the road, deployed to the right and left of the road, the right extending to the crest of the hill and the left stretching out into the open field. Over this open ground the line steadily advanced, under a heavy infantry and artillery fire, and drove the enemy from their strong and covered position on the hills.[6]

Leaving your parking place on the Loop Road, return through Liberty Gap. As you enter the gap notice a small log house on the right after traveling 0.80 mile. This was the headquarters of Colonel Featherston. After 1.30 miles note the house on the left, which was the headquarters of General Willich at the end of the first day of fighting. The 1863 road that existed in 1863 ran in front of the house, while the modern road on which you are driving is behind the house.

When you have driven 1.80 miles, turn left on a small unnamed road—the 1863 road. After 400 yards stop at a T-intersection, parking on the shoulder. In front of you and to the south is the position the Confederates held on June 25 and 26. Turn around, and you will see the position the Union forces held on the same days. You are standing about halfway between the opposing lines.

On June 25–26, 1863, the field where you are standing was covered in knee-high cornstalks, and it was the scene of heavy skirmishing as Union and Confederate units moved forward to take position. Since McCook had been ordered to make only a feint, no serious Union attack was mounted. The Confederates were waiting to respond to any Union move.

At this location the sharpshooters trained by Maj. Gen. Patrick Cleburne went into action using Whitworth rifles. Union officers reported taking losses from shots fired from an estimated one-thousand-yard range, and Cleburne independently supported that conclusion.

Report of Maj. Gen. Patrick Cleburne, Commanding Division, Hardee's Corps

The enemy kept up a constant firing all day, the 26th, and advanced twice with double lines of skirmishers. They were driven back, and at night both parties held their former positions. I had no ammunition to spare, and did not reply to the continual fire of the enemy except with five Whitworth rifles, which appeared to do good service. Mounted men were struck at distances ranging from 700 to 1300 yards.[7]

From your parking spot turn right (west), and return in a short distance to SR 269. Turn left (south) and go back to Bell Buckle. At the center of town turn left on SR 82, then return to SR 64. Turn right (south) on SR 64, and proceed to Wartrace.

Fairfield is 3.30 miles from the turn onto SR 64. Notice the historical marker on the right of the road. The camp of the division commanded by Maj. Gen. A. P. Stewart, Fairfield is also the point from which Bate's Brigade marched for Hoover's Gap.

Stop 5—Wartrace

On reaching Wartrace, which is 4.30 miles from Fairfield, park in the area in front of the businesses, walk across the railroad, and turn right on the street in front of the Walking Horse Hotel. The third building is Chockley's Tavern (privately occupied) and was the headquarters of Patrick Cleburne. Across the street from the tavern is a kiosk with maps and information concerning the Tullahoma Campaign.

Wartrace was an important rail junction in 1863 because the branch line to Shelbyville, headquarters of Polk's Corps, met the main line of the Nashville & Chattanooga Railroad, which led east to army headquarters in Tullahoma.

Quote from Lieut. Col. Arthur James Lyon Fremantle

1st June. A soldier was shot in Wartrace this afternoon. We heard the volley just as we left in the cars for Shelbyville. His crime was desertion to the enemy; and as the prisoner's brigade was at Tullahoma (twenty miles off), he was executed without ceremony by the provost guard. Spies are hung every now and then; but General Bragg told me it was almost impossible for either side to stop the practice.[8]

Stop 6—Tullahoma

Return to your car, and continue on SR 64 toward Shelbyville. At a four-way stop (5.30 miles from Wartrace) turn left on SR 347. At a stop sign in 0.20 mile, turn left (south) on US 41A toward Tullahoma.

On entering Tullahoma. US 41A is signposted Jackson Street. Continue on Jackson Street (US 41A) for a total of 13.50 miles to West Decherd Street. (Landmarks—Methodist Church, Post Office, then three blocks.). Turn right, and immediately turn left to enter rounds of South Jackson Civic Center. Park in the provided area.

This spot was the headquarters encampment of the Army of Tennessee from January to July 1863. Here Lieutenant General Bragg made most of his critical decisions affecting the Tullahoma Campaign. The area was covered with tents, and approximately 250 men worked in this location as clerks and administrators of various army departments. Warehouses and buildings used as hospitals stood across Jackson Street, reaching as far as the railroad two blocks away.

Looking toward Jackson Street you will see a stone marker, an information kiosk, and several metal historical markers describing the events of the Tullahoma Campaign that occurred near this site. Visit the markers and kiosk before returning to your car.

Stop 7—Estill Springs Railroad Bridge

Return to your car, and go back to US 41A (Jackson Street). Turn right (south) on Jackson Street and proceed 7.90 miles to Estill Springs. The 1863 road no longer exists, but it was located on the opposite side of the railroad tracks. The present road was constructed in the 1920s.

On reaching Estill Springs pass through three traffic lights, and then watch for a left turn into the Estill Springs City Park. Drive to the end of the park road, and exit your car. The railroad bridge in front of you is in the same location as the 1863 bridge. The river crossing here was defended by troops of Benjamin F. Cheatham's troops defended the river crossing here on July 1–2, 1863; Philip Sheridan's troops crossed downstream at a ford on July 3.

On leaving the park, turn left and cross the bridge. Immediately on the left is a historical marker for the location of Camp Harris, a site used by Judge Peter Turney to raise troops for the Confederacy even before Tennessee left the union. In 1863 the camp was the recruiting and training center for the Sixteenth US Colored Troops.

Stop 8—Decherd Depot Site

On reaching Decherd, 4.20 miles away, turn left on Main Street, and continue for 0.80 mile. Just before crossing the railroad tracks turn left into the public park. In 1863 the Decherd Depot stood directly in front of you as you face the tracks. The stockade protecting the depot was just behind your left shoulder on the slight hill. Wilder struck this spot on June 28, burning the depot and destroying the water tank and three hundred yards of track.

> Our Colonel has invented a simple little thing to tear up railroad track and to twist it so they cannot be put down again. It looks like an over-sized horseshoe with flanges on the ends. We hook it under the rail and take our hatchets and cut a lever and get a pry in it from across the rail with a rope at the top of the pole. Eight of us can jerk the iron right up.[9]

Stop 9—Winchester

Leave the park, and return to US 41A. Turn left at the junction with the highway, then follow US 41A into Winchester.

The city limits of Decherd and Winchester join so that there is no obvious division between the two towns. Follow US 41A around the courthouse, and proceed south. After 3.40 miles you will cross Boiling Fork Creek. The 1863 road is just to the right of the modern street. The rear guard of Wheeler's cavalry and the advance guard of Sheridan's Division fought a skirmish here.

To view the 1863 stream crossing turn right (west) at the first street across

Boiling Fork Creek, and then look to the right. You may then return to US 41A.

Stop 10—Cowan

From Boiling Fork Creek drive 4.30 miles to Cowan. Cross the railroad, immediately turn right, and park in the spaces provided. The public park provides a good view toward the mountains, which are penetrated by the 2,200-foot Cowan Tunnel. The tunnel cannot be accessed by road or by foot. Cowan was the site of the Army of Tennessee's final encampment before retreating to Chattanooga.

Across the tracks from your parking spot is a small museum of railroad memorabilia that some will find interesting.

The following story persists: As the last Confederates retreated through the streets of Cowan, an old woman chased the cavalrymen with a broom, scolding them for running. "If ole Forrest was here he'd make y'all fight!" she is reputed to have said, never realizing she was shouting at Forrest. Unfortunately for the story, Forrest was at Monteagle, and Joe Wheeler commanded the retreating cavalry.

Stop 11—Sewanee

After leaving Cowan continue on US 41A up the mountain. The 1863 road was about 1.0 south of you and is not passable. On reaching the top of the mountain, a distance of 5.80 miles, stop at the intersection with SR 56, and read the historical marker. The 1863 road joined the modern route at this point, as did the branch line of the railroad that ran to Tracy City. A running skirmish was fought from this point back to the campus of the University of the South.

Col. Louis D. Watkins led the Fifth and Sixth Kentucky Cavalry (USA) up the mountain from Cowan, while the Eighth Texas and the Fourth Tennessee under Lieut. Col. Paul Anderson contested their advance. The clash of these cavalrymen on the morning of July 4 marked the end of the Tullahoma Campaign.

Letter from Robert Franklin Bunting, Chaplain, Terry's Texas Rangers, Eighth Texas

Companies D, K, and H were in advance. . . . Thus things stood during the night of the 3rd. After sun up in the mornng, the enemy,

> who had stood picket on the brow of the mountain, advanced in sweeping charge, cutting off H and driving K back upon D. The guns of K mostly missed fire, and the whole mass together fell back upon D, which was in line of battle.
>
> The enemy charged up within five paces, when he received a volley which drove him back 400 yards, being closely followed by D. The enemy here being in strong force Captain Kyle ordered his gallant company to fall back to their original position where they reformed, and as the enemy advanced he charged him again and the 2d time drove him back. D and K were frequently mixed up with the enemy, and it was a hand to hand fight and very severe.[10]

Continue on US 41A to the first traffic light, turn left, and drive through the campus of the University of the South, founded just prior to the war by, among others, Bishop Leonidas Polk. Polk returned to the campus on July 3, 1863, as a Confederate lieutenant general.

The drive through the campus brings you back to US 41A. Turn left (east) at the stop sign. After passing through the stone gateposts marking the end of the university domain, drive 0.40 mile, and look to the right for a road signposted "Midway." This was the route Polk's Corps followed as it retreated to Chattanooga.

Continue ahead to Monteagle and a junction with I-24. There are motels, restaurants, and other facilities here. This completes your tour.

APPENDIX II

UNION ORDER OF BATTLE

ARMY OF THE CUMBERLAND
Maj. Gen. William S. Rosecrans

FOURTEENTH ARMY CORPS
Maj. Gen. George H. Thomas

FIRST DIVISION
Maj. Gen. Lovell H. Rousseau

First Brigade
Col. Benjamin F. Scribner
38th Indiana
2nd Ohio
94th Ohio
10th Wisconsin

Second Brigade
Col. Henry A. Hamabright
24th Illinois
79th Pennsylvania
1st Wisconsin
21st Wisconsin

Third Brigade

Brig. Gen. John H. King
15th United States, 1st Battalion
16th United States, 1st Battalion
18th United States, 2nd Battalion
19th United States, 1st Battalion

Artillery

Col. Cyrus O. Loomis
4th Indiana
1st Michigan
5th United States, Battery H

SECOND DIVISION

Maj. Gen. James S. Negley

First Brigade

Brig. Gen. John Beatty
104th Illinois
42nd Indiana
88th Indiana
15th Kentucky
3rd Ohio

Second Brigade

Col. William L. Stoughton
19th Illinois
11th Michigan
18th Ohio
69th Ohio

Third Brigade

Col. William Sirwell
37th Indiana
21st Ohio
74th Ohio
78th Pennsylvania

Artillery

Capt. Frederick Schultz
2nd Kentucky Battery
1st Ohio, Battery G
1st Ohio, Battery M

THIRD DIVISION

Brig. Gen. John M. Brannon

First Brigade

Col. Moses B. Walker
82nd Indiana
17th Ohio
31st Ohio
38th Ohio

Second Brigade

Brig. Gen. James B. Steedman
10th Indiana
74th Indiana
4th Kentucky
10th Kentucky
14th Ohio

Third Brigade

Col. Ferdinand Van Derveer
87th Indiana
2nd Minnesota
9th Ohio
35th Ohio

Artillery

4th Michigan Battery
1st Ohio, Company C
4th United States, Company I

FOURTH DIVISION

Maj. Gen. Joseph J. Reynolds

First Brigade

Col. John T. Wilder
18th Illinois
123rd Illinois
17th Indiana
72nd Indiana

Second Brigade

Col. Albert S. Hall
80th Illinois

68th Indiana
75th Indiana
101st Indiana
105th Ohio

Third Brigade
Brig. Gen. George Crook
18th Kentucky
11th Ohio
36th Ohio
89th Ohio
92nd Ohio

Artillery
18th Indiana Battery
19th Indiana Battery
21st Indiana Battery

TWENTIETH ARMY CORPS

Maj. Gen. Alexander McD. McCook

FIRST DIVISION

Brig. Gen. Jefferson C. Davis

First Brigade
Col. P. Sidney Post
59th Illinois
74th Illinois
75th Illinois
22nd Indiana

Second Brigade
Brig. Gen. William P. Carlin
21st Illinois
38th Illinois
81st Illinois
101st Ohio

Third Brigade
Col. Hans C. Heg
25th Illinois
35th Illinois
8th Kansas
15th Wisconsin

Artillery

2nd Minnesota Battery
5th Wisconsin Battery
8th Wisconsin Battery

SECOND DIVISION

Brig. Gen. Richard W. Johnson

First Brigade

Brig. Gen. August Willich
89th Illinois
32nd Indiana
39th Indiana
15th Ohio
49th Ohio

Second Brigade

Col. Joseph B. Dodge
34th Illinois
79th Illinois
29th Indiana
30th Indiana
77th Pennsylvania

Third Brigade

Col. Philemon P. Baldwin
6th Indiana
5th Kentucky
1st Ohio
93rd Ohio

Artillery

Capt. Peter Simonson
5th Indiana Battery
1st Ohio Battery
20th Ohio Battery

THIRD DIVISION

Maj. Gen. Philip H. Sheridan

First Brigade

Brig. Gen. William H. Lytle
36th Illinois

88th Illinois
21st Michigan
24th Wisconsin

Second Brigade
Col. Bernard Laiboldt
44th Illinois
73rd Illinois
2nd Missouri
15th Missouri

Third Brigade
Col. Luther P. Bradley
22nd Illinois
27th Illinois
42nd Illinois
51st Illinois

Artillery
Capt. Henry Hescock
1st Illinois, Battery C
11th Indiana Battery
1st Missouri, Battery G

TWENTY-FIRST ARMY CORPS

Maj. Gen. Thomas L. Crittenden

FIRST DIVISION

Brig. Gen. Thomas J. Wood

First Brigade
Col. George P. Buell
100th Illinois
58th Indiana
13th Michigan
26th Ohio

Second Brigade
Brig. Gen. George D. Wagner
15th Indiana
40th Indiana
57th Indiana
97th Ohio

Third Brigade
Col. Charles G. Harker
3rd Kentucky
64th Ohio
65th Ohio
125th Ohio

Artillery
Capt. Cullen Bradley
8th Indiana Light Battery
10th Indiana Light Battery
6th Ohio Light Battery

SECOND DIVISION
Maj. Gen. John M. Palmer

First Brigade
Brig. Gen. Charles Cruft
31st Indiana
1st Kentucky
3rd Kentucky
90th Ohio

Second Brigade
Brig. Gen. William B. Hazen
9th Indiana
6th Kentucky
41st Ohio
124th Ohio

Third Brigade
Col. William Gorse
84th Illinois
36th Indiana
23rd Kentucky
24th Ohio

Artillery
Capt. William E. Standart
1st Ohio, Battery B
1st Ohio, Battery F
4th United States, Battery H
4th United States, Battery M
110th Illinois Battalion—Unassigned

THIRD DIVISION
Brig. Gen. Horatio P. Van Cleve

First Brigade
Brig. Gen. Samuel Beatty
79th Indiana
9th Kentucky
17th Kentucky
19th Ohio

Second Brigade
Col. George F. Dick
44th Indiana
86th Indiana
13th Ohio
59th Ohio

Third Brigade
Col. Sidney M. Barnes
35th Indiana
8th Kentucky
21st Kentucky
51st Ohio
99th Ohio

Artillery
Capt. Lucius H. Drury
7th Indiana Battery
Independent Pennsylvania Battery B
3rd Wisconsin Battery

RESERVE CORPS
Maj. Gen. Gordon Granger

FIRST DIVISION
Brig. Gen. Absalom Baird

First Brigade
Col. Smith D. Atkins
92nd Illinois
96th Illinois
115th Illinois

84th Indiana
40th Ohio

Second Brigade
Col. William P. Reid
78th Illinois
98th Ohio
113th Ohio
121st Ohio

Third Brigade
Col. Henry C. Gilbert
33rd Indiana
19th Michigan

Artillery
1st Illinois, Battery M
9th Ohio Battery
18th Ohio Battery

SECOND DIVISION

Brig. Gen. James D. Morgan

First Brigade
Col. Robert F. Smith
10th Illinois
16th Illinois
60th Illinois
10th Michigan
14th Michigan

Second Brigade
Col. Daniel McCook
85th Illinois
86th Illinois
125th Illinois
52nd Ohio

Third Brigade
Col. Charles C. Doolittle
18th Michigan
22nd Michigan
106th Ohio
108th Ohio

Artillery

2nd Illinois, Battery I
1st Ohio, Battery E
10th Wisconsin Battery

THIRD DIVISION

Brig. Gen. Robert S. Granger

First Brigade

Col. William P. Lyon
83rd Illinois
71st Ohio
13th Wisconsin
2nd Illinois Artillery, Battery C
2nd Illinois Artillery, Battery H

Second Brigade

Brig. Gen. William T. Ward
102nd Illinois
105th Illinois
129th Illinois
70th Indiana
79th Ohio
5th Michigan Battery

CAVALRY CORPS

Maj. Gen. David S. Stanley

FIRST CAVALRY DIVISION

Brig. Gen. Robert B. Mitchell

First Brigade

Col. Archibald P. Campbell
4th Kentucky
6th Kentucky
7th Kentucky
9th Pennsylvania
1st Tennessee

Second Brigade

Col. Edward M. McCook
2nd Indiana

4th Indiana
5th Kentucky
2nd Tennessee
1st Wisconsin
1st Ohio Artillery

SECOND CAVALRY DIVISION
Brig. Gen. John B. Turchin

First Brigade
Col. Robert H. G. Minty
3rd Indiana
5th Iowa
4th Michigan
7th Pennsylvania
4th United States
1st Ohio Battery

Second Brigade
Col. Eli Long
2nd Kentucky
1st Ohio
3rd Ohio
4th Ohio
10th Ohio
Stokes's Illinois Battery

APPENDIX III

CONFEDERATE ORDER OF BATTLE

THE ARMY OF TENNESSEE
Lieut. Gen. Braxton Bragg

POLK'S ARMY CORPS
Lieut. Gen. Leonidas Polk

CHEATHAM'S DIVISION
Maj. Gen. Benjamin F. Cheatham

Maney's Brigade
Col. J. A. McMurry
1st and 27th Tennessee
4th Tennessee
6th and 9th Tennessee
24th Tennessee Battalion
Smith's Mississippi Battery

Smith's Brigade
Brig. Gen. Preston Smith
11th Tennessee
12th and 47th Tennessee
13th and 154th Tennessee

29th Tennessee
Scott's Tennessee Battery

Wright's Brigade
Col. John H. Anderson
8th Tennessee
16th Tennessee
28th Tennessee
51st Tennessee
Carnes's Battery

Strahl's Brigade
Col. O. F. Strahl
19th Tennessee
24th Tennessee
31st Tennessee
29th Tennessee
Stanford's Battery

WITHERS'S DIVISION

Maj. Gen. Jones M. Withers

Anderson's Brigade
Brig. Gen. Patton Anderson
7th Mississippi
9th Mississippi
10th Mississippi
44th Mississippi
9th Mississippi Battalion
Robertson's Battery

Deas's Brigade
Col. J. G. Coltart
19th Alabama
22nd Alabama
25th Alabama
50th Alabama
17th Alabama Battalion
Garrity's Battery

Walthall's Brigade
Brig. Gen. E. C. Walthall
24th Mississippi

27th Mississippi
29th Mississippi
30th Mississippi
34th Mississippi
Fowler's Battery

Manigault's Brigade
Brig. Gen. A. M. Manigault
24th Alabama
28th Alabama
34th Alabama
10th and 19th South Carolina
Water's Battery

HARDEE'S ARMY CORPS
Lieut. Gen. William J. Hardee

CLEBURNE'S DIVISION
Maj. Gen. Patrick R. Cleburne

Wood's Brigade
Col. M. P. Lowrey
16th Alabama
33rd Alabama
45th Alabama
32nd and 45th Mississippi
Sharpshooters
Semple's Battery

Churchill's Brigade
Brig. Gen. T. H. Churchill
19th and 24th Alabama
6th, 10th, and 15th Texas
17th, 18th, 24th, and 25th Texas
Douglas's Battery

Liddell's Brigade
Brig. Gen. St. John Liddell
2nd Arkansas
5th Arkansas
6th and 7th Arkansas
8th Arkansas

13th and 15th Arkansas
Swett's Battery

Polk's Brigade
Brig. Gen. L .E. Polk
1st Arkansas
3rd and 5th Confederate
2nd Tennessee
35th Tennessee
48th Tennessee
Calvert's Battery

STEWART'S DIVISION

Maj. Gen. Alexander P. Stewart

Johnson's Brigade
Brig. Gen. Bushrod R. Johnson
17th Tennessee
23rd Tennessee
25th Tennessee
44th Tennessee
Darden's Battery

Brown's Brigade
Brig. Gen. John C. Brown
18th Tennessee
26th Tennessee
32nd Tennessee
45th Tennessee
23rd Tennessee Battalion
Dawson's Battery

Bate's Brigade
Brig. Gen. William B. Bate
9th Alabama
4th Georgia Battalion Sharpshooters
37th Georgia
15th and 37th Tennessee
20th Tennessee
Eufaula Battery

Clayton's Brigade
Brig. Gen. H. D. Clayton
18th Alabama

36th Alabama
38th Alabama
Humphrey's Battery

Jackson's Brigade
Brig. Gen. John K. Jackson
1st Confederate
2nd Georgia Battalion Sharpshooters
5th Georgia
5th Mississippi
8th Mississippi
Pritchard's Battery
Scoggin's Battery

CAVALRY CORPS

Maj. Gen. Joseph Wheeler

WHARTON'S DIVISION

Brig. Gen. John A. Wharton

Crews's Brigade
Col. C. C. Crews
7th Alabama
2nd Georgia
3rd Georgia
4th Georgia

Harrison's Brigade
Col. Thomas Harrison
1st Confederate
1st Kentucky (a.k.a. 3rd)
4th Tennessee (a.k.a. 8th)
8th Texas
11th Texas

Artillery
White's Battery

MARTIN'S DIVISION

Brig. Gen. Will T. Martin

Hagan's Brigade
Col. James Hagan

1st Alabama
3rd Alabama
8th Confederate

Russell's Brigade
Col. A. A. Russell
4th Alabama
1st Confederate
Wiggins's Battery

MORGAN'S DIVISION

Brig. Gen. John H. Morgan

Duke's Brigade
Col. Basil W. Duke
2nd Kentucky
5th Kentucky
6th Kentucky
9th Kentucky
9th Tennessee

Cluke's Brigade
Col. R. S. Cluke
8th Kentucky
10th Kentucky
Chenault's Regiment
Gano's Regiment

Artillery
Byrne's Battery

FORREST'S DIVISION

Brig. Gen. Nathan B. Forrest

Armstrong's Brigade
Brig. Gen. Frank C. Armstrong
3rd Arkansas
2nd Kentucky
McDonald's Battalion

Cox's Brigade
Col. Nicholas N. Cox
4th Tennessee

8th Tennessee (a.k.a. 13th)
9th Tennessee (a.k.a. 19th)
10th Tennessee
11th Tennessee

Artillery
Freeman's Battery
Morton's Battery

Artillery Reserve
Col. James Deshler
1st Louisiana Battery
Lumsden's Battery
Massenburg's Battery
Havis's Battery
Barrett's Battery
Orleans Guard Artillery

NOTES

Preface

1. Phil Leigh, "Why Minnesota Chose Civil War," Civil War Chat, July 12, 2018, www.civilwarchat.com.
2. Michael R. Bradley, *Tullahoma: The 1863 Campaign for Control of Middle Tennessee.* (Shippensburg, PA: Burd Street Press, 2000). This monograph covers the period from January to July 1863, including a day-by-day account of the ten days of the Tullahoma Campaign.

   Arthur James Lyon Fremantle, *The Fremantle Diary* (1864; repr., Short Hills, NJ: Burford Books, 1954). This is a travel journal kept by Lt. Col. James Fremantle, who visited the Army of Tennessee in June 1863, just days before the active phase of the Tullahoma Campaign began. The book contains a description of generals and an account of a review of a Confederate brigade, the only eyewitness description of the dress and armament of Army of Tennessee troops from the period.

   Earl J. Hess, *Braxton Bragg: The Most Hated Man of the Confederacy* (Chapel Hill: University of North Carolina Press, 2016). Hess devotes a chapter to the Tullahoma Campaign and Bragg's relations with his subordinate generals as well as to the state of Bragg's health.

   Christopher L. Kolakowski, *The Stones River and Tullahoma Campaigns.* (Charleston, SC: History Press, 2011). The author presents the Tullahoma Campaign as a postlude to Stones River and a prelude to Chickamauga.

William M. Lamers, *The Edge of Glory: A Biography of General William S. Rosecrans, U.S.A.* (Baton Rouge: Louisiana State University Press, 1999). This well-written biography of Rosecrans devotes a chapter to the Tullahoma Campaign, showing that Rosecrans felt his accomplishments to have been largely overlooked.

Glenn W. Sunderland, *Lightning at Hoover's Gap: The Story of Wilder's Brigade in the Civil War* (New York: Thomas Yoseloff, 1969). This well-written and thoroughly researched account of Wilder's Brigade focuses on the mounted infantrymen's organization and arming at the time of the Tullahoma Campaign, but it also includes an account of the rest of the unit's service.

Steven E. Woodworth, *Six Armies in Tennessee: The Chickamauga and Chattanooga Campaigns.* (Lincoln: University of Nebraska Press, 1998). Woodworth includes several references to the Tullahoma Campaign as setting the stage for the Chickamauga and Chattanooga operations.3. Larry Peterson, *Decisions at Chattanooga* (Knoxville: University of Tennessee Press, 2018); Matt Spruill and Lee Spruill, *Decisions at Stones River* (Knoxville: University of Tennessee Press, 2018); Matt Spruill & Matt Spruill IV, *Decisions at Second Manassas* (Knoxville: University of Tennessee Press, 2018).

Introduction

1. Lamers, *Edge of Glory*, 258–60, 267.
2. James McPherson, *For Cause and Comrades: Why Men Fought in the Civil War* (New York: Oxford University Press, 1997) 122–23; Mark E. Neely Jr., *The Fate of Liberty*, (New York: Oxford University Press, 1991), 60–61; Michael L. Leonard, *Civil War Letters, Ohio Soldiers of Hancock County, 21st Ohio Vols. and 49th Ohio Vols.* (Aurora, CO: Privately Printed, 1995), 18; Dennis W. Belcher, *General David S. Stanley: A Civil War Biography* (Jefferson, NC: McFarland, 2014), 2.
3. US War Department, *The Official Records of the War of the Rebellion: A Compilation of the Official Records of the Union and Confederate Armies*, 70 volumes in 128 parts (Washington, DC: US Government Printing Office, 1880–1901), series 1, vol. 23, pt. 2, pp. 618, 625–26. I, 23, 2, 18, 287, 290–91, 527. (This source is hereinafter cited as *OR*.)
4. James A. Connolly, *Three Years in the Army of the Cumberland: 1862–1865.* (Baton Rouge: Louisiana State University Press, 1959), 58.
5. Hess, *Braxton Bragg*, 114–15, passim.

6. Bradley, *Tullahoma*, 18–19.
7. US Supreme Court associate justice John Catron maintained a summer cottage in Tullahoma that both armies used, in turn, as a headquarters. Catron was one of the five justices ruling with the majority in the Dred Scott case, but he stayed in the North throughout the Civil War and retained his seat on the court.
8. *OR*, ser. 1, vol. 23, pt. 2, p. 821; Thomas Lawrence Connelly, *Autumn of Glory: The Army of Tennessee, 1862–1865* (Baton Rouge: Louisiana State University Press, 1971), 115.
9. Connelly, *Autumn of Glory*, 762ff.
10. Edgar Longacre, *A Soldier to the Last: Maj. Gen. Joseph Wheeler in Blue and Gray* (Washington, DC: Potomac Books, 2007), 87–89.
11. Ibid., 91–94; Jack Hurst, *Nathan Bedford Forrest: A Biography* (New York: Alfred A. Knopf, 1993), 113–16; Brian Steel Wills, *A Battle from the Start: The Life of Nathan Bedford Forrest* (New York: HarperCollins, 1992), 97–102; Lonnie Maness, *An Untutored Genius: The Military Career of General Nathan Bedford Forrest* (Oxford, MS: Guild Bindery Press, 1990), 119.
12. *OR*, ser. 1, vol. 23, pt. 1, pp. 86–87, 116–17; Maness, *Untutored Genius*, 123–27.
13. *OR*, ser. 1, vol. 23, pt. 1, pp. 287–91 chronicles the pursuit and capture of Streight. Virtually every biography of Forrest examines this event as well.
14. A good account of this episode is in John Allan Wyeth, *That Devil Forrest: Life of General Nathan Bedford Forrest* (1899; repr., Baton Rouge: Louisiana State University Press, 1959), 200–202.
15. John Fitch, *Annals of the Army of the Cumberland* (Philadelphia: J. B. Lippincott, 1864), 425–36; James A. Ramage, *Rebel Raider: The Life of General John Hunt Morgan* (Lexington: University Press of Kentucky, 1986), 151–53; Sunderland, *Lightning at Hoover's Gap*, 100–104.

Chapter 1

1. *OR*, ser. 1, vol. 23, pt. 2, pp. 618, 625–26; Hess, *Braxton Bragg*, 100–101. The text of the note from the generals can be found in *OR*, ser. 1, vol. 20, pt. 1, pp. 700–702. Kolakowski, *Stones River and Tullahoma Campaigns*, 88–89.

2. *OR*, ser. 1, vol. 23, pt. 1, pp. 73, 625–26, 688–89.
3. Bradley, *Tullahoma*, 19–20.
4. Michael R. Bradley, *The Raiding Winter* (Gretna, LA: Pelican, 2013), 109–10.
5. Lamers, *Edge of Glory*, 249.
6. Abraham Lincoln to William S. Rosecrans, letter dated January 5, 1863 in *The Collected Works of Abraham Lincoln*, ed. Roy P. Basler (New Brunswick, NJ: 1953), 6:424.
7. Leonard E. Brown, "Fortress Rosecrans: A History," *Tennessee Historical Quarterly* 50, no. 3 (Fall 1991): 136–67.
8. John C. Spence, *Annals of Rutherford County*, Vol. 2, *1829–1870*. *Publications of the Rutherford County Historical Society* (Murfreesboro, TN: The Society) Vol. 39, 152.
9. Brown, "Fortress Rosecrans," 138. See also Michael R. Bradley and Shirley Jones, *Murfreesboro in the Civil War* (Charleston, SC: History Press, 2012), chapter 5; and Larry J. Daniel, *Days of Glory: The Army of the Cumberland, 1861–1865* (Baton Rouge: Louisiana State University Press, 2004), 235.
10. Daniel, *Days of Glory*, 234.
11. William M. Lamers, *The Edge of Glory: A Biography of General William S. Rosecrans* (Baton Rouge: Louisiana State University Press, 1999), 253
12. Ibid., 254.
13. The only significant use of cavalry in the Vicksburg Campaign was the raid made by Benjamin Grierson. He was opposed by only two regiments of Confederate cavalry and scattered home guard and state troop units.
14. *OR*, ser. 1, vol. 23, pt. 2, pp. 45, 95; Bradley, *Tullahoma*, 27.
15. Sunderland, *Lightning at Hoover's Gap*, 17–19.
16. Connelly, *Autumn of Glory*, 81.
17. Ibid., 81; Hess, *Braxton Bragg*, 133.
18. Richard A. Baumgartner, *Blue Lightning: Wilder's Mounted Infantry Brigade in the Battle of Chickamauga* (Huntington, WV: Blue Acorn, 2007), 63; Sunderland, *Lightning at Hoover's Gap*, 28–29.
19. Baumgartner, *Blue Lightning*; Sunderland, *Lightning at Hoover's Gap*, 29.
20. Wyeth, *That Devil Forrest*, 200–201; Maness, *Untutored Genius*, 52.

21. Woodworth, *Six Armies in Tennessee*, 33; *OR*, ser. 1, vol. 23, pt. 1, p. 618; Connelly, *Autumn of Glory*, 117.
22. Betty J. Gorin, *"Morgan Is Coming!": Confederate Raiders in the Heartland of Kentucky* (Louisville: Harmony House, 2006), 100; Bradley, *Tullahoma*, 44.
23. Basil W. Duke, *History of Morgan's Cavalry* (Miami, OH: Miami Printing Company, 1867; repr., Columbus, OH: General Books, 2009), 226.
24. Virginia L. French, entry for February 15, 1863, in *Diary* (Privately printed by Jerry Smith, n.d.), 66–67.
25. Ramage, *Rebel Raider*, 160. Fitch, *Annals*, 434–36.
26. W. C. Dodson, ed., *Campaigns of Wheeler and His Cavalry: 1862–1865* (Atlanta: Hudgins, 1899; repr., E. F. Williams and J. J. Fox, 1997), 85.
27. Bradley, *Tullahoma*, 57, 58, 80.
28. Lammers, *Edge of Glory*, 278.
29. Belcher, *General David S. Stanley*, 132–35.

Chapter 2

1. Bradley, *Tullahoma*, 59; Kolakowski, *Stones River and Tullahoma Campaigns*, 110–11; *OR*, ser. 1, vol. 23, pt. 1, pp. 425, 466–67, 608.
2. Lamers, *Edge of Glory*, 277–78; John W. Rowell, *Yankee Artilleryman: Through the Civil War with Eli Lilly's Indiana Battery* (Knoxville: University of Tennessee Press, 1986), 84; Benjamin F. Magee, *History of the 72nd Indiana Volunteer Infantry of the Mounted Lightning Brigade* (LaFayette, IN: S. Vater, 1882; repr., Huntington, WV: Blue Acorn, 1992), 128–29.
3. Bradley, *Tullahoma*, 84; *OR*, ser. 1, vol. 23, pt. 1, pp. 621–22, 891.
4. Daniel, *Days of Glory*, 269; Baumgartner, *Blue Lightning*, 49–51; Connolly, *Three Years*, 90–94; Rowell, *Yankee Artilleryman*, 84; *OR*, ser. 1, vol. 23, pt. 1, pp. 430, 442, 457–59.
5. *OR*, ser. 1, vol. 23, pt. 1, p. 524; Lamers, *Edge of Glory*, 283.
6. *OR*, ser. 1, vol. 23, pt. 1, pp. 521, 580.
7. Ibid., ser. 1, vol. 23, pt. 1, 583, 618–19.
8. Ibid., ser. 1, vol. 23, pt. 1, pp. 425, 466–67, 608; Bradley, *Tullahoma*, 80.
9. Rowell, *Yankee Artilleryman*, 84.

10. Bradley, *Tullahoma*, 84; *OR*, ser. 1, vol. 23, pt. 1, pp. 621–22, 891.
11. *OR*, ser. 1, vol. 23, pt. 1, p. 619.
12. Ibid., ser. 1, vol. 23, pt. 1, pp. 622–23; Harold B. Simpson, ed., *The Bugle Softly Blows: The Confederate Diary of Benjamin M. Seaton* (Waco, TX: Texian Press, 1965), 35.
13. Bradley, *Tullahoma*, 86; Kolakowski, *Stones River and Tullahoma Campaigns*, 134.
14. Bradley, *Tullahoma*, 87; Kolakowski, *The Stones River and Tullahoma Campaigns*, 135.
15. Merritt R. Blakeslee, "A Right Sharp Little Fight," *Sewanee: Alumni & Friends of the University of the South Magazine*, Winter 2014, 24–29.

Chapter 3

1. Michael R. Bradley, *With Blood and Fire: Life Behind Union Lines in Middle Tennessee, 1863–65* (Shippensburg, PA: Burd Street Press, 2003), 194–95; Bradley, *Tullahoma*, 90–91.
2. *OR*, ser. 1, vol. 23, pt. 2, pp. 517, 521, 525, 526–27; Union Provost Marshal Files, microfilm, MC 345, Roll 89, Tennessee State Library and Archives, Nashville.
3. Hess, *Braxton Bragg*, 150; Grady McWhiney and Judith Lee Hallock, *Braxton Bragg and Confederate Defeat* (Tuscaloosa: University of Alabama Press, 1991), 2:32–33.
4. *OR*, ser. 1, vol. 23, pt. 2, p. 518; Baumgartner, *Blue Lightning*, 116. At one point Stanton's insistence that Rosecrans advance immediately led Rosecrans to offer to resign his command.
5. McWhiney and Hallock, *Braxton Bragg and Confederate Defeat*, 2:14–15.
6. Ibid., 2:36, 40–41.
7. Ibid., 2:40.

Appendix I

1. Spence, *Annals of Rutherford County*, 2:83, 85.
2. *OR*, ser. 1, vol. 23, pt. 1, p. 612.
3. Connolly, *Three Years*, 67.
4. Fremantle, *Fremantle Diary*, 123–25.

5. *OR*, ser. 1, vol. 23, pt. 1, p. 587.
6. Ibid., ser. 1, vol. 23, pt. 1, p. 507.
7. Ibid., ser. 1, vol. 23, pt. 1, p. 586.
8. Fremantle, *Fremantle Diary*, 125–26.
9. Baumgartner, *Blue Lightning*, 93.
10. Thomas W. Cutrer, ed., *Our Trust Is in the God of Battles: The Civil War Letters of Robert Franklin Bunting, Chaplain, Terry's Texas Rangers, C.S.A.* (Knoxville: University of Tennessee Press, 2006), 171.

BIBLIOGRAPHY

Basler, Roy P. *The Collected Works of Abraham Lincoln*. 8 vols. New Brunswick, NJ: 1953.

Baumgartner, Richard A. *Blue Lightning: Wilder's Mounted Infantry Brigade in the Battle of Chickamauga*. Huntington, WV: Blue Acorn, 2007.

Belcher, Dennis W. *General David S. Stanley: A Civil War Biography*. Jefferson, NC: McFarland, 2014.

Blakeslee, Merritt R. "A Right Sharp Little Fight." *Sewanee Alumni & Friends Magazine of the University of the South*, Winter 2014.

Bradley, Michael R. *The Raiding Winter*. Gretna, LA: Pelican, 2013.

———. *Tullahoma: The 1863 Campaign for Control of Middle Tennessee*. Shippensburg, PA: Burd Street Press, 2000.

———. *With Blood and Fire: Life Behind Union Lines in Middle Tennessee, 1863–65*. Shippensburg, PA: Burd Street Press, 2003.

Bradley, Michael R., and Shirley Jones. *Murfreesboro in the Civil War*. Charleston, SC: History Press, 2012.

Brown, Leonard E. "Fortress Rosecrans: A History." *Tennessee Historical Quarterly* 50, no. 3 (Fall 1991).

Connelly, Thomas Lawrence. *Autumn of Glory: The Army of Tennessee, 1862–1865*. Baton Rouge: Louisiana State University Press, 1971.

Connolly, James A. *Three Years in the Army of the Cumberland*. Bloomington: Indiana University Press, 1959.

Cooling, Benjamin Franklin. *Fort Donelson's Legacy: War and Society in Kentucky and Tennessee, 1862–1863*. Knoxville: University of Tennessee Press, 1997.

Cutrer, Thomas W., ed. *Our Trust Is in the God of Battles: The Civil War Letters of Robert Franklin Bunting, Chaplain, Terry's Texas Rangers, C.S.A.* Knoxville: University of Tennessee Press, 2006.

Daniel, Larry J. *Days of Glory: The Army of the Cumberland, 1861–1865*. Baton Rouge: Louisiana State University Press Press, 2004.

Dodson, W. C., ed. *Campaigns of Wheeler and His Cavalry, 1862–1865*. Atlanta: Hudgins, 1899. Reprint. E. F. Williams and J. J. Fox, 1997.

Duke, Basil W. *History of Morgan's Cavalry*. Miami, OH: Miami Printing Company, 1867. Reprint. General Books, 2009.

Fitch, John. *Annals of the Army of the Cumberland*. Philadelphia: J. B. Lippincott, 1864.

Fremantle, Arthur James Lyon. *The Fremantle Diary*. 1864. Reprint. Short Hills, NJ: Buford Books, 1954.

French, Virginia L. *Diary*. Privately printed by Jerry Smith, n.d.

Gorin, Betty. *"Morgan Is Coming!": Confederate Raiders in the Heartland of Kentucky*. Louisville: Harmony House, 2006.

Hess, Earl J. *Braxton Bragg: The Most Hated Man of the Confederacy*. Chapel Hill: University of North Carolina Press, 2016.

Hurst, Jack. *Nathan Bedford Forrest: A Biography*. New York: Alfred A. Knopf, 1993.

Kolakowski, Christopher. *The Stones River and Tullahoma Campaigns*. Charleston, SC: History Press, 2011.

Lamers, William M. *The Edge of Glory: A Biography of General William S. Rosecrans, U.S.A.* Baton Rouge: Louisiana State University Press, 1999.

Leonard, Michael L. *Civil War Letters, Ohio Soldiers of Hancock County 21st Ohio Vols. and 49th Ohio Vols*. Aurora, CO: Privately printed, 1995.

Longacre, Edward G. *A Soldier to the Last: Maj. Gen. Joseph Wheeler in Blue and Gray*. Washington, DC: Potomac Books, 2007.

Magee, Benjamin F. *History of the 72nd Indiana Volunteer Infantry of the Mounted Lightning Brigade*. Lafayette, IN: S. Vater, 1882. Reprint. Huntington, WV: Blue Acorn, 1992.

Maness, Lonnie. *An Untutored Genius: The Military Career of General Nathan Bedford Forrest*. Oxford, MS: Guild Bindery Press, 1990.

McPherson, James. *For Cause and Comrades: Why Men Fought in the Civil War.* New York: Oxford University Press, 1997.

McWhiney, Grady, and Judith Lee Hallock. *Braxton Bragg and Confederate Defeat.* 2 vols. Tuscaloosa: University of Alabama Press, 1991.

Neely, Mark, Jr. *The Fate of Liberty: Abraham Lincoln and Civil Liberties.* New York: Oxford University Press, 1991.

Peterson, Larry. *Decisions at Chattanooga.* Knoxville: University of Tennessee Press, 2018.

Ramage, James A. *Rebel Raider: The Life of General John Hunt Morgan.* Lexington: University Press of Kentucky, 1986.

Rowell, John W. *Yankee Artilleryman: Through the Civil War with Eli Lilly's Indiana Battery.* Knoxville: University of Tennessee Press, 1986.

Simpson, Harold B., ed. *The Bugle Softly Blows: The Confederate Diary of Benjamin M. Seaton.* Waco, TX: Texian Press, 1965.

Spence, John C. *Annals of Rutherford County.* Vol. 2, *1829–1870. Publications of the Rutherford County Historical Society,* Vol. 39. Murfreesboro, TN: Rutherford County Historical Society.

Spruill, Matt, and Lee Spruill. *Decisions at Stones River.* Knoxville: University of Tennessee Press, 2018.

Spruill, Matt, and Matt Spruill IV. *Decisions at Second Manassas.* Knoxville: University of Tennessee Press, 2018.

Sunderland, Glenn W. *Lightning at Hoover's Gap: The Story of Wilder's Brigade in the Civil War.* New York: Thomas Yoseloff, 1969.

Union Provost Marshal Files. Microfilm. Tennessee State Library and Archives, Nashville.

US War Department. Official Records of the War of the Rebellion: A Compilation of the Official Records of the Union and Confederate Armies. 70 volumes in 128 parts. Washington, DC: US Government Printing Office, 1880–1901.

Wills, Brian Steel. *A Battle from the Start: The Life of Nathan Bedford Forrest.* New York: HarperCollins, 1992.

Woodworth, Steven E. *Six Armies in Tennessee: The Chickamauga and Chattanooga Campaigns.* Lincoln: University of Nebraska Press, 1998.

Wyeth, John Allan. *That Devil Forrest: Life of General Nathan Bedford Forrest.* 1899. Reprint. Baton Rouge: Louisiana State University Press, 1959.

INDEX